Withdrawn from Stock
Dublin City Public Libraries

An Easter People

Essays In Honour of
Sr Stanislaus Kennedy

D1390628

Edited by John Scally

VERITAS

First published 2005 by
Veritas Publications
7/8 Lower Abbey Street
Dublin 1
Ireland
Email publications@veritas.ie
Website www.veritas.ie

10 9 8 7 6 5 4 3 2 1

ISBN 1 85390 857 6

Copyright © The individual contributors, 2005

The material in this publication is protected by copyright law.
Except as may be permitted by law, no part of the material may be
reproduced (including by storage in a retrieval system) or
transmitted in any form or by any means, adapted, rented or lent
without the written permission of the copyright owners.
Applications for permissions should be addressed to the publisher.

A catalogue record for this book is available from the British Library.

Designed and Typeset by Paula Ryan
Printed in the Republic of Ireland by Betaprint, Dublin

*Veritas books are printed on paper made from the wood pulp of managed
forests. For every tree felled, at least one tree is planted, thereby renewing
natural resources.*

Very special thanks to all the contributors who so generously gave of their time to write the essays and poems. Thanks to Bloodaxe Books for permission to use the six Brendan Kennelly poems. Thanks to Maura Hyland, Helen Carr, Daragh Reddin and all at Veritas for their enthusiastic support of this book.

CONTENTS

CONTRIBUTORS

An Taoiseach, Bertie Ahern TD is, among other things, Ireland's best-known Manchester United fan.

Eavan Boland is one of Ireland's most distinguished poets and she has won a number of prestigious awards. Her collections include *Outside History*, *Object Lessons* and *In A Time of Violence*.

Lelia Doolan has worked in theatre, television, film and journalism as a producer/director, writer and teacher. She is formerly the Artistic Director of the Abbey Theatre and Chairman of Bord Scannan na hEireann/the Irish Film Board. She took part in the early days of Combat Poverty. She participated in the campaign to restore the site at Mullaghmore in Clare. She contributes to a number of publications.

Ursula Halligan is TV3's political correspondent and is the winner of numerous awards for her journalism. She presents the current affairs and politics programme *The Political Party* on TV3.

In 1997, at the age of twenty, **Denis Hickie** made his senior debut for Ireland, and he has gone on to become one of Ireland's most celebrated rugby players.

Brendan Kennelly is Ireland's best-loved poet. He was Professor of Modern Literature at Trinity College, Dublin for thirty years, and retired from teaching in 2004. He has published over twenty books of poetry. He is the only living writer to have a literary festival in his name. He marked his retirement from Trinity College with the publication of *Familiar Strangers: New and Selected Poems 1960-2004*, a personal selection of work from his forty-four years as a poet.

Gordon Linney is the former Church of Ireland Archdeacon of Dublin. He is married with three grown-up children and lives in Glenageary, County Dublin.

Sarah McDonald has been a contributor to religious publications for a number of years and is an acclaimed radio documentary-maker. She currently edits *The Word* magazine.

Peter McVerry is a Jesuit priest. For years he has championed the cause of the marginalised in Irish society. He is particularly associated with the campaign to provide accommodation for homeless boys.

John O'Donohue came to international prominence with the publication of his book *Anam Cara: Spiritual Wisdom from the Celtic World*. It became a publishing phenomenon and remained on the best-seller list for two years. He is a philosopher and poet and holds a doctorate in philosophical theology from the University of Tübingen. His other publications include *Person als Vermittlung*, a study of Hegel and *Divine Beauty: The Invisible Embrace*, Transworld, 2004.

Helena O'Riordan Keleher graduated with a degree in Biblical and Theological Studies from Trinity College Dublin in 2003. She currently works in the Department of Enterprise, Trade and Employment while pursuing a Post-graduate Diploma in Conflict and Dispute Resolution Studies at the Irish School of Ecumenics.

Micheal O'Siadhail has published a number of collections of poetry, which include *The Gossamer Wall, Hail! Madam Jazz* and *A Fragile City.* Awarded an Irish-American Cultural Institute Prize for poetry in 1981 and the Marten Toonder Prize for Literature in 1998, he has read and broadcast his poetry widely in Ireland, Britain, Europe, North America and Japan.

Ruairi Quinn, TD, is an architect and town planner who graduated from UCD in 1969. Elected to the Dail in 1977, he is the Labour deputy for Dublin South-East. He has been Minister for Labour, the Public Service, Enterprise and Employment and Finance. He was leader of the Labour Party from 1997 to 2002 and is currently spokesperson on European Affairs and is Treasurer of the Party of European Socialists.

Trevor Sargent, TD, is the leader of the Green Party. He is an active member of the Church of Ireland. He also has a keen interest in the Irish language.

A native of Roscommon, **John Scally** is Beresford Lecturer in Ecclesiastical History in the School of Religions and Theology in Trinity College, Dublin. His books include: *Whose Death is it Anyway?: Euthanasia and the Right to Die; After the Brave New World?: Ethics and Genetics* and *Doctor's Orders?: Towards a New Medical Ethics.*

Kathy Sinnott describes her life in two phases BJ and AJ – 'Before Jamie' and 'After Jamie'. Her son Jamie was only three months old when he first began to exhibit symptoms of autism. For twenty-five years Kathy has campaigned to ensure that no more young people will ever have to 'share the scrapheap with Jamie' and, like him, arrive at the age of eighteen uneducated. In 2004 she was elected to the European Parliament.

Alice Taylor was born on a farm near Newmarket in County Cork. She worked as a telephonist in Killarney and Bandon until she married, when she moved to Innishannon. She ran a guesthouse at first, then the local supermarket and post office. She and her husband, Gabriel Murphy, have four sons and one daughter. *To School Through the Fields,* her first book of memoirs of country life quickly became one of the biggest-selling books ever published in Ireland. Her sequels, *Quench the Lamp, The Village, Country Days* and *The Night Before Christmas* also captured the pulse and sinews of rural Ireland and topped the bestsellers charts.

FOREWORD

An Taoiseach, Mr Bertie Ahern TD

It is remarkable when an individual makes an impact on public life by changing our understanding of some aspect of the society in which we live. It is even more remarkable when that understanding is matched by initiatives that make a real difference to the quality of life in society.

What is truly remarkable about Sr Stanislaus Kennedy is that she has had this impact not once or twice, but on a number of occasions. She has been a prophetic voice, ahead of her time in recognising issues which must be addressed and innovating new ways of engaging with them. Many will recall her pioneering work in Kilkenny with the legendary Bishop Birch. That work has had a lasting impact on social service provision and the voluntary sector in Ireland. Subsequently, her work with the homeless and more recently with migrants has provided new insights and stimulated new responses from Irish society.

Her public impact has extended beyond the area of social provision, however. She has been a distinguished member of the Council of State. She is a successful author and has inspired many to develop their spiritual life.

I suspect that it is her reaching out to people through her writing, as well as through the development of a spiritual retreat in her inner-city convent, which gives her most satisfaction. Because, fundamentally, Stan is a Sister of Charity. Her whole personality reflects that. It informs her vision and underpins her tireless effort. It is that characteristic, which, I suspect, impresses all of those on whom she calls for support and which makes co-operation in her projects irresistible.

Even when she has critical things to say – and I have heard them on many occasions – she does it in a way, which affirms the individual and points towards an achievable and better future.

Campaigning can be a negative experience for all concerned. Even when it brings success, it can polarise and alienate. In her public work, Stan has been a positive campaigner, even when, at least for a time, she has been a lone voice.

It is right that we should celebrate and treasure those who help to make us better people. As a society, we have grown sceptical of heroes and heroines, never mind saints. I am happy to salute the exceptional life and contribution of Stan and to wish her many more years to 'comfort the afflicted and afflict the comfortable'.

Bertie Ahern TD
An Taoiseach

PREFACE

Denis Hickie

I always admired Sr Stanislaus Kennedy and the work she does for the poor and those on the margins of Irish society.

When I was approached to become a patron of an organisation she set up called the Young Social Innovators, I was delighted to do so. It is a project targeted at transition year students in Ireland. Like the Young Scientists, the Young Social Innovators are asked to examine an issue of interest to them and find a solution. They look at instances of social injustice and dream up original ways to solve them. I got the chance to visit their exhibition and saw the great work so many students do right across the country to help people less fortunate than themselves. I think when young people get involved in this way at an early age some of that concern stays with them. In a country where we focus more on what we can do and get for ourselves, YSI not only makes young people more aware of the social issues that affect everybody in Ireland, but also provides the support to make their solutions a reality. From my own experiences of sport I know how important it is to tap into young people's idealism and nurture it.

Of course, Sr Stan is best known for her work with Focus Ireland where she has done such great work for the many homeless people in our country. She has made a real difference to so many people for so long.

I am delighted that all royalties from this book are going to Focus Ireland; by buying this book you will help Sr Stan to continue to make a difference. I hope you will enjoy it.

INTRODUCTION

John Scally

Sr Stanislaus Kennedy has made it her mission in life to bring in as many people as possible from the margins of Irish society, and to robustly critique the system that causes people to live on the margins in the first place. Down through the years she has held up a mirror to Irish society and sometimes we could only wince at what we saw in the reflection. As the Taoiseach, Bertie Ahern, acknowledges in the Foreword she has repeatedly questioned – in her own uniquely forthright way – why some have an unacceptable standard of living, and has consistently pointed to the need to improve the quality of life for everyone who is on the breadline, even when others might have liked her to keep quiet. What she has consistently provided us with is a relentlessly well-polished looking-glass positioned at an uncomfortably close angle to show us the inequalities in our society.

She has performed an invaluable service to us by enabling us to see more clearly what we have become. She has dared us as a society to ask questions we would rather have avoided and made us look at ourselves in communal self-examination. She not only steers us to a national examination of conscience, but also dares us to engage in a national examination of *consciousness*, in order to reclaim and relearn the values that we pledge our adherence to.

In the Ireland of today there are many possible responses to the injustices in society. One might be a prophet denouncing the evils of the age and announcing a better age to come. Alternatively, one could be a preserver, making sure that in the flux of life the validity of past insights is not lost. Sr Stan, in word and deed, incarnates a third approach: to share the drama of our age and work for the advancement of society and the common good.

This book was conceived to pay tribute to a remarkable woman who has made a significant contribution to Irish public life and Irish Christianity. Knowing that all royalties of the book go to Focus Ireland, each of the contributors to this volume has been inspired by Sr Stan and, rather than pay homage to her directly, they have been invited to reflect on a topic with which she has some involvement. Many of them chose to do so in an indirect fashion. In this way *An Easter People* will hopefully be a modest contribution to raising public debate about many of the issues she has been associated with: homelessness, the experience of immigrants and asylum-seekers in Ireland, justice and inequality in all its forms, encouraging young people, and the nature of Christianity today, to name but a few.

John Scally
February 2005

THE GOOD

Brendan Kennelly

Brendan Kennelly was the first person to agree to contribute to the book. His poems are scattered throughout this collection. In conversation with me he explained his interest in the idea of An Easter People. *'I am fascinated by Christianity and the figure of Christ. I constantly marvel at the fact that those who are followers of Christianity believe that even before we were born and long after we die, there is at work a provident, gracious God who has created us and loves us and wants us to share in His own life. This view shapes the Christian's moral life by enabling them to live in faith, in hope and in love. Accordingly, Christianity issues us with an invitation into the heart of what it is to be human. I love the idea of the divinisation being most tellingly revealed by our humanisation.*

'Of course as someone who has spent a lifetime studying – in various ways – words, I particularly admire the statement in the Gospel: "In the beginning was the Word and the Word was with God and the Word was God".

'I love the idea of a religion that is based on love which is best summed up in the quotation from St Paul, "To live through love in God's presence." Every day I open the papers and I read stories about the absence of love in the world and it depresses me.

'Love of God is expressed not only in prayer and Sunday worship, but must permeate every aspect of our lives. The Bible has no

ambiguities on one issue: you cannot love God unless you love your neighbour. The Old Testament prophets were scathing in their cititcism of those who sought to appraise God by prayers and sacrifices while oppressing the powerless. Jesus told us that all the law and the prophets are summarised in the commandment to love God and the neighbour. No words are minced when we are told: "Whoever claims to love God but hates his brother or sister is a liar." (I Jn 4:20)

'All love invites love. God calls us to love. I am enthralled by the compassion of God and Jesus to people. There are days when I'm very far away from this, but I'm always inspired by the image of Jesus in the Gospels. He was someone who brought the compassion of God to people, someone who didn't judge or condemn. He was someone who was with people wherever they were, especially those who found themselves on the margins of society. One of the things that really interests me is the nature of goodness. I think people who reach out to those in need best sum it up. I wrote a poem called 'The Good' and I think these type of people embody all that goodness is.'

The Good

The good are vulnerable
As any bird in flight,
They do not think of safety,
Are blind to possible extinction
And when most vulnerable
Are most themselves.
The good are real as the sun,
Are best perceived through clouds
Of casual corruption
That cannot kill the luminous sufficiency
That shines on city, sea and wilderness,

Fastidiously revealing
One man to another,
Who yet will not accept
Responsibilities of light.
The good incline to praise,
To have the knack of seeing that
The best is not destroyed
Although forever threatened.
The good go naked in all weathers,
And by their nakedness rebuke
The small protective sanities
That hide men from themselves.
The good are difficult to see
Though open, rare, destructible;
Always, they retain a kind of youth,
The vulnerable grace
Of any bird in flight,
Content to be itself,
Accomplished master and potential victim,
Accepting what the earth or sky intends.
I think that I know one or two
Among my friends.

TOWARDS A POETICS OF POSSIBILITY

John O'Donohue

Organisations like Focus Ireland *consistently remind us that despite all the wealth created since the boom of 'the Celtic Tiger' Irish society continues to be afflicted with major social and economic problems. Although material poverty is a fact of life for a significant number of people, for many of us the poverty is spiritual, a poverty of love or imagination. Often we are so preoccupied with the world as it is that we forget the Ireland that might be. In both his essay and his poem John O'Donohue celebrates the world of possibility and in the process challenges us to embark on an imaginative quest to rediscover our spititual centre.*

The visible world exerts a magnetic force on the eye; in a thousand tugs of colour, shape and direction, vision is claimed by the visible, offering everywhere the familiar surprise of things. The world as seen by the eye furnishes the central images that dominate how we think and what we see. This quiet harvesting of the visible provides us with anchor and shelter in the world. It follows us inward to the furthest rooms of interiority. And even at night, when we close our eyes, we close out the visible only to find it already there, awaiting us within, in dream. With the emergence of the eye, the self gained its inner mirror wherein the difference and the distance of things could arrive and appear in the intimacy of image. It is little wonder that in perception the eye enjoys a magnificent primacy. When it dwells on the diversity and depth of the visible, perception is always confronted by immense vistas. Yet our addiction to the visible blinds us to the other adjacent worlds that nourish and sustain the world we see.

The Invisible World

There is a special world adjacent to us that we rarely consider. Without its presence, generosity and passion, our actual world would be pale, numb and empty. This world rarely draws attention to itself. It subsists in silence. Though the actual world owes it everything, it is never tempted to push it aside in order to emerge and claim the light for itself. Attention and exploration it never seems to encourage. Yet no thing, no form, no colour, no animal, plant, no ocean, star or human being could ever have emerged without the infinite fecundity, limitless creativity and unbounded generosity of that world. This is the world of possibility.

The world of possibility is silent, yet dense with the dreams of what could be. The world we normally inhabit is an abbreviated world, a world selected from that prior realm of plenitude. Most lives articulate and unfold themselves through a unique sequence of experience. This sequence is never broken; it has a continuity which sustains itself through the ordinary run of days and nights and often through the most abysmal ruptures and visitations of strangeness. A review of a life usually considers the facts of experience, the thresholds, the situations and the people who participated with us along the way. We take this to be the real material of our lives; it becomes the mirror that allows us to glimpse who we are and what meaning our lives have. The facts of what we have lived stand out. We take them as given and real. Yet all these facts have issued from that huge adjacency of possibility, that neighbouring world that shimmers invisibly behind all that we take to be real.

Only when we are faced with choice, do we consider the presence of possibility and the invitations that it offers. Possibilities come alive for us when we find ourselves on a threshold where new directions signal to us. This experience is seldom and we tend to look back on such moments of decision as times when character became galvanised through willed choice and action. Normally, we never notice how the penumbral realm of possibility is actually the artistic milieu that offers us a subtle diversity in order to compose what we think, how we see and act and informs the depth and extent of who we choose to become.

Possibility As Genesis

In the beginning was the possibility. Without it was made nothing of all that was made. Before anything could be, it first had to be possible. Everything had its genesis in possibility. Rather than viewing possibility as the realm of genesis, we tend to register it but occasionally, and then merely as the realm of the alternative; whereas in actual fact, possibility signifies that underlying matrix of potential that is always present, and from which every single thing derives. In contrast to the arena of the possible, the domain of fact assumes sureness and definiteness; this is evident in the difference between the language of fact and the language of possibility. Demonstrative words signpost the indisputable giveness of fact: 'Here it is', 'There it is', 'The situation is', 'The case is such', 'The thing is clear', 'We have established the facts', 'The fact of the matter', 'Hard facts', 'The evidence is conclusive', 'We have a witness who saw the whole thing', 'We can say without a doubt'. This language is one of description, giveness and occurrence. In contrast, the language of possibility always seems tenuous: 'Anything is possible', 'Unfortunately, it remains only in the realm of possibility', 'And maybe she will come', 'None of that is clear yet', 'It is still a vague possibility'. Actuality is seen as that which is real in itself; whereas when we say something is possible, we mean it might or might not happen, but its becoming cannot be assured. It might well occur if certain conditions accrue or fall into place. Fact does not have to work to gain our attention or convince us; it seems to have the confidence to wait for us to recognise it. Fact indicates what is, what is stable and real.

In philosophy, possibility is a modal concept, a characteristic it shares with necessity. Nothing necessary is impossible. '*Anake*' is the Greek world for 'necessity'; it played a huge role in Greek thought. Near the end of the classical period Macrobius wrote: '*Amor osculo significatur, neccesitas nodo*', that is, 'Love is represented with a kiss, necessity with a knot.'

Nothing impossible is necessary. Possibility is thus often profiled over against the concept of impossibility. We speak of contingency when something is not impossible and yet not necessary. In early Greek philosophy, in the Presocratics, philosophy had the sense of '*dunamis*' or capacity. Here at the infancy of the Western discursive tradition, there was a profound sense of the kinetic interaction of elemental forces as affording a glimpse into that nexus between the origin and unfolding of the world. For Plato, '*dunamis*' or possibility was at the heart of the subject's call to knowing and ethical responsibility. Plato was never concerned with knowledge as a possession, but with the struggle to know as the pathway to truth, wisdom and goodness.

When the root of possibility was sought in actuality, the Stoics recognised the danger in drawing the realm of the possibility too close to the actual; it began to take on the strain of too much concrete reality and was in danger of becoming over determined. The purity and freedom of possibility diminished in the neighbourhood of the actual. The Stoics were also aware that the extent and multiplicity of possibility could never be fully exhausted or grasped by understanding. Even the most inclusive epistemology could always only select from the dense matrix, only partial moments could be rendered explicit, all else was left unthematised. Early reflection came to recognise that the realm of the possible had an intense kinship with time and its stages. Reflection on future possibility or prognosis had to remain, of necessity, always provisional. The past and the present offered more hospitable access as the conditions of their eventuality were already given. The past cannot be forced to un-happen: you cannot un-ring a bell.

Possibility In Aristotle

This sense of the kinetic world where possibility dwells found fascinating portrayal in the thought of Aristotle. The fundamental architecture of his philosophy was built with the concepts of possibility-actuality, *'dunamis-energeia'*, potency and act. The phenomenon of change and movement led Aristotle to analyse possibility. Whatever was emerging or becoming was analysed in terms of its arrival point, its goal which is *'eidos'* or *'energeia'*. Considered in terms of emerging reality, that which is not yet real may still be possible; though over against possibility, reality enjoyed ontological primacy. In the process of the realisation of a thing potentialities played a key role. Whereas a passive potency could set the condition of a thing happening, it was the active potency that drove its realisation towards reality. While the whole world is in a constant flow of movement and change, each concrete worldly reality is permeated with possibility. Understanding reality as the domain of *'energeia'*, he was fascinated by how something becomes. What conditions must prevail on the threshold for something to become?

Aristotle's thinking was a kinetic philosophy of becoming; the fascination was directed primarily towards the 'not yet'. Reality dwelt in being as possibility. From the beginning, then, possibility was not merely an imagined theoretical construct to ground the source of emergence and arrival, it was also seen as a matrix of living force which urged things into existence, then infused existence with relentless invitations to actualise what was 'not yet'. Possibility became the living bridge between the 'already' and the 'not yet' both in the domain of being and of existential choice and becoming. Aristotle showed that possibility and actuality are relational concepts. He offers no definition of possibility in and for itself; he chooses rather to use it as a tool to interpret what unfolds in concrete reality. In relation to the philosophy of possibility, there is no transition from the ontological to the logical in Aristotle.

The Scholastic View and Kant

The concept of possibility underwent a sea-change with the advent of Scholastic thought. The doctrine of *'creatio ex nihilo'* shifted the analysis of possibility from the consideration of becoming *in* the world to the becoming *of* the world itself. Possibility was now employed in the endeavour to conceptualise the world as a whole; this hinged on the understanding of God as creator. The omnipotence of God now becomes the absolute creative source from whence possibility issues. The concrete actuality of the world is the expression of the Thought of God; the possibilities within the divine imagination is where everything comes from. The ontological source is the *'pleroma'*, the abundance of divine fullness that imbues creation with possibility not merely in an originary sense, but also as in Meister Eckhart with the sense of *'creatio continua'*. Actuality is the agency of permanent and sustaining divine possibility.

Later Leibniz brought the theory of possibility deeper into the frame of logic and human cognition. Beginning with the classical recognition that possibility is that which is not contradictory, Leibniz went on to claim that space and time are the pure ideal frames for the ordering of possible things. However, it was left to Kant to develop a transcendental philosophy that would articulate the creative cognitional power of possibility in experience. Kant draws a key distinction between what is logically possible and what is really possible. This is the distinction between what we can think and what it is possible for us to objectively know. He problematises the notion of giveness. Objects are given to sense knowing within the persistent frames of time and space. Experience is the ground of our knowing. Finite understanding is not in a position to grasp the concepts of things in the conditions of their possibility.

Kant evokes a sense of the vast matrix of possibility which underlies grounds and enables our perception. Both the world and the subject have an inbuilt capacity and need for coherence that come alive together to allow us to know. Thus, we cannot simply read coherence and meaning from the raw imprint of sensation on the intellect. Neither can we simply attribute coherence to sensation from some a priori categories given by the intellect. Rather both arise together when the act of knowing begins to actualise itself. This is the birth point of the famous synthetic a priori. It is the wedding of the subjectivist and objectivist traditions. Neither alone would have yielded this. Kant's transcendental method, then, renders explicit the very conditions of the possibility of knowing and unearths the profound unity of subject and world, and their mutual necessity in the act of knowing. The object in Kant is not the stand-alone object of the rationalist, the object seems to be already oriented towards the subject and the subject is not the stand-alone, all-construcivist subject of Idealism. Kant managed to clear and evoke a middle ground, the transcendental condition-of-possibility ground where the actuality of their unity becomes active and explicit; he puts possibility at the heart of the philosophy of knowing.

The Question As The Custodian of Possibility

Philosophical reflection is itself an incredible and creative possibility. Without doctrinal restriction or ideological bias, it has the freedom to attempt a clearance where – to use Mallarmé's famous phrase – 'the white page' might receive the mirroring of the subtle structures of what is and what could be. In this freedom, philosophy can attempt a genesis-geography and portrayal of the oblique spaces between word and thing, silence and sound, being and consciousness. Though often caricatured as abstraction, this can in fact develop into a speculative poetry of Being. The joy of such thought is the extent of its scope and the intensity of its penetration. The burden of such thought is its duty of integrity to bend and circle with the radical reflexivity of it own self-mirroring and questioning. It is thought which is always at pains to pursue and reflect its own reflexivity. Such thought can never be a one dimensional covering or merely composed collage. Its faithfulness is, as Plato said, to follow the question wherever it leads in this restless yet passionate marriage of mutuality between the epistemological and the ontological.

Possibility in philosophical reflection emerges and comes to expression in the question. The question is the mirror where the unknown becomes visible as critical and unveiling possibility. The question is the subtle custodian of possibility and philosophy is the province where the question is king. The fecundity of possibility comes to light in the question whose desire is to break the grip of the static fixation into which giveness so easily and continuously falls. The beauty and infuriation of philosophy is how the question remains permanently hungry and open. Great questions never settle to sleep inside answers. The question can open and come alive at any point thus rendering philosophical space permanently tense and elegantly strained.

Since philosophy is continually fuelled by the question, it can never settle. A philosophical text is a tense force-field circulating continually around the hunger of the question. This is why the problem of beginning has been such a fecund threshold all through the history of philosophical reflection: where to begin? How to begin? What to begin with? The question is the space where thought is most alert to its source and its possibility. The dream of thought is to enfold totality. Gadamer speaks beautifully of beginning as Incipience: 'Being incipient refers to something that is not yet determined in the direction of this or that sense, not yet determined in the direction of this or that end, and not yet determined appropriate for this or that representation. This means that many eventualities are still possible.' He says 'it is a setting out without knowledge, the goal of an emanation rich in possibilities.' The question, the beginning is the adventure on the pathway where new possibilities emerge towards an ever increasing determinedness and concrescence.

Possibility Activates A Force-Field of Change

Philosophy shares this longing with experience: the desire for the New. This is not the New as the latest banal fashion or accidental appearance; it has rather a depth and substance that distinguishes itself from that which is simply different or other. It has an inner relationship to that which is of value and has emerged and established itself in the memory and history of a society's spirit-substance. The New, in this sense, does not emerge frequently, yet the desire for the New is one of the deepest longings of consciousness and especially of consciousness as spirit. The loyalty of the true question is always towards the clearance and critique that can allow and invite the Novum to emerge. Its arrival becomes an invitation to deeper integration and wholeness. In this sense, one could claim that the desire of possibility is wholeness.

In the elucidation of possibility as the invitation to wholeness, one must be careful not to hypostasise possibility into some kind of adjacent and self-completed singular guest who simply enters with a pre-arranged gift. Too frequently our perception tends to be a single shot perception which views possibility in a single cylinder way: one thing is possible, one thing enters into the firing pin of actualisation and that is it, then perception moves on from the passed thing. Possibility is, however, a more multifarious and subtly structured, indeed, webbed presence. It invokes and invites the whole person to actualisation, calling upon the full force of the faculties of thought, feeling, will and imagination. This involves difficulty, recognition and perseverance. The limitations and fixation of giveness is not to be simply overthrown by the elegant arrival of an already complete and self-assured possibility; rather possibility alerts and activates the diverse force-field of consciousness and intentionality. This is how possibility can be truly transformative and effect prophetic change. There is an interesting passage in Bernard Lonergan's *Insight* which speaks to this: 'Basically, then, finality is the dynamic aspect of the real. To affirm finality is to disagree with the Eleatic negation of change. It is to deny that this universe is inert, static, finished, complete. It is to affirm fluidity, tension, approximativeness, and incompleteness. It is an affirmation that may turn out to have implications for the future, but such implications are a further question, for finality is an affirmation of fact and fact pertains not to the future but to the present and the past.'

Following this elucidation of the dynamic invitation intrinsic to finality, Lonergan goes on to explicate possibility as an inner tension of opposites that drives being to transcend limits: 'It follows that potency is a tension of opposites. As we have seen, it is the ground of universal limitation; as we have just added, it is the ground of the finality that carries proportionate being ever beyond actual limitations. However, this does not mean that potency is a contradictory notion, for contradiction arises only when mutually exclusive predicates are attributed to the same object under the same aspect. In potency there are at least two aspects of its proper contribution to the constitution of proportionate being and, on the other hand, its relation to the other contributions of form and act. The proper contribution of potency is limitation. But the relation of potency to the other contributions is general and indeterminate, yet dynamic and directed towards such contributions. It is the indeterminacy of that directed dynamism that makes potency the principle of the tendency to transcend limitations.'

The Drama of Facts and Possibilities
The consideration of possibility as a force of transformative invitation enables us to re-cast our perspective on what facts

actually are. Facts are not as lonely as they appear. Possibility is the mother of fact. Each fact is a former possibility. A fact emerges from a cluster of possibilities; it is a possibility that has been actualized. As soon as a fact confronts us, it seems to absorb all our attention, it is, after all, a live, engaging thing. One of the most encouraging methods to effect change in a fixated situation is to probe behind its surface facticity and pierce through to the mother-cluster of possibility from which it originally emerged. Visiting this matrix of originary possibility can awaken unnoticed energy behind numbed facticity and render a situation fluent and creative again. There are always endless possibilities secretly present in situations that seem prima facie frozen.

Experience is a panorama of latent possibility; there is a multiplicity of unknown possibilities that will never be thought, seen or engaged. On which threshold does possibility most frequently emerge? This is a fascinating existential question that lends itself to endless enumeration. It does seem, however, that wherever there is awakening and openness, possibility is more likely to emerge and become apparent. But possibility can also awaken when time fractures at moments of crisis or *kairos*; pressure can press out possibility. Generally, it does seem that wherever life has become reduced, narrow and frozen, possibility is more difficult to discern and engage; frequently, for those who live inside such confinement, there seems to be absolutely no possibility. Life is simply as it is; it can never become other.

An interesting question in this nexus where fact emerges from possibility is to ask what happens to the other sister possibilities that for a moment hovered in the vicinity of realisation and emergence, were near being chosen but then were not. Is there a repository somewhere of un-chosen possibilities which were left stranded as one of their number became the chosen one for the coveted position in the light? Where do un-chosen possibilities dwell? Do they remain in some interim limbo, in some kind of pre-existential arrest? Do un-actualised possibilities simply disperse and re-assemble in other clusters to circulate again near the frontiers of choice and actualisation? Or do past clusters from which a fact has grown hold their form, and perhaps in this way secretly accompany and sustain the pilgrimage of their colleague in the domain of facticity? At an existential level, each of us is the one we are now because of certain possibilities we chose on certain key thresholds. The lives we have chosen fashion us into who we are. What became of the lives that were once possibilities for us but remained un-chosen? Did they disappear and dissolve? Or did they, perhaps, in a secret way accompany us and realise themselves on their own terms? Where do our un-chosen lives dwell? The excavation and retrieval of this matrix of unlived possibility calls the imagination to engage memory.

The Invisible Sanctuary of Memory

In the existential biography of human subjectivity there is no threshold more creative than that between memory and possibility. Though possibility is always hovering near, and experience is the arena where possibility is realised, the future of every experience is still disappearance. Transience makes a ghost of experience. Human life is a threshold where lived experience is continually falling away and vanishing. One of the key questions of identity is: where do these experiences go? As the Medievals put it: where does the flame go when the candle is quenched? Is there a place where our vanished days secretly gather? Perhaps there is and the name of that place is memory. Experience is the continual conversion of possibility into memory.

While experiences vanish, memory remains. Indeed, the narrative of an individual life is the secret construction of this invisible sanctuary of memory. This is where all the known and unknown substance of our days and nights is gathered and selected until it finds the form of memory. This is subtle imaginative work. Memory is not merely the reception of the raw imprint of experience nor its simple storage. There is a harvesting imagination that works at the heart of memory which searches the lived substance of our days until it clarifies and settles into a form that abides. Almost without our noticing it, the individual sanctuary of memory is forever finding its way further into structure and shape. This work continues until the substance of our last hours on earth is received into its deeper lived form. When at last the body falls and the visible life vanishes, the finished sanctuary of memory holds all the harvested possibility.

Evanescence and Memory in Hegel

Hegel's philosophical system is full of movement, change and becoming. At its heart is a vigorous philosophy of possibility. The Hegelian dialectic is not an external method to be subsequently applied to experience. For Hegel, the dialectic is the inner rhythm of experience that spurs it to unfold its latent possibility. Experience is a constant unfolding and thematising of possibility towards its depths and extremes until it yields new frontiers where extremity and opposition become transfigured and enexpected new possibilities emerge to call the journey into deeper creativity. Underlying the courage and vulnerable openness of the dialectic is a subtle philosophy of memory according to which nothing is ever lost or forgotten. It was Hegel's epic achievement in speculative thought to uncover the secret network of bridges where consciousness is linked to history. Central to this is the recognition that experience is the continual transfiguration of possibility into memory and that memory in turn is the harvest repository from which the new springtime of possibility flowers forth: 'The goal is Spirit's insight into what knowing is... the *length* of this path has to be endured, because, for one thing, each moment is necessary; and further, each moment has to be *lingered* over, because each is itself a complete individual shape... the content is already the actuality reduced to possibility, its immediacy overcome, and the embodied shape reduced to abbreviated, simple determinations of thought... it is... existence... now recollected in-itself, ready for conversion into the form of being-for-self.'

And speaking of transience, Hegel says: 'The evanescent itself must, on the contrary, be regarded as essential... appearance is the arising and passing away that does not itself arise and pass away, but is "in-itself" and constitutes the actuality and the movement of truth. The True is the Bacchanalian revel in which no member is not drunk; yet because each member collapses as soon as he drops out, the revel is just as much transparent as simple repose.' According to Hegel then, actuality is reduced to possibility and this is at the heart of the life of truth. Memory is the transfigured harvest of gathered and realised possibility, the secret imagination of time where experience becomes Spirit.

Imagination and Possibility

The beauty of possibility resides both in its creative urgency and in its hospitality to all forms and rhythms of experience. The Western thought tradition awakened with the Greeks. Their elucidation of the Soul and the Logos uncovered a seam of brightness that shines through all their philosophy. But that brightness was nearly always too intense for the life of the senses and the integrity of bodily individuality to claim their space. They rarely achieved a worthy conceptual portraiture; they inevitably appeared in blurred and shadowed form. Even when Christianity emerged, it tended to articulate itself in these dualistic terms, even though the informing axiom of the Incarnation demanded portraiture of individuality as the inviolable and intimate unity of divinity and humanity. This dualistic strain has dominated the Western mind. It has tended to freeze the porous threshold at the heart of natural duality, thus producing a destructive dualism that falsely divided reality into separate zones. This placed a savage burden on human subjectivity, forcing it to endure along false territories of inner and outer exile. In itself, duality is the call to creativity and wholeness. Duality is the inner conversation of life with itself. The threshold of duality runs right through these sister dimensions: light/dark, known/unknown, fact/possibility, before/ after, inside/outside, above/below, beginning/ending, identity/change, silence/word, masculine/feminine, thought/ feeling, senses/soul, self/other and human/divine. The divided mind separates each from the other and can never participate in the challenge and journey of their conversation, conflict and creativity.

Only the imagination feels and follows the call to the justice of wholeness. The imagination is the great friend of possibility. Where the imagination is alive, fixated positions cannot claim final authority. Giveness is not allowed to proclaim any despotism of fact. The eye of the imagination always keeps adjacent and latent possibility in view and is drawn to engage with its desire and direction. The beauty of imagination is its openness to novelty. New possibility has permission to invite it anywhere. Neither is possibility rigged or pre-set in terms of where it wants to awaken or which form it desires to invite. Furthermore, imagination is inevitably drawn to energy and disturbance; consequently, it is ideally poised to explore and excavate the awkward thresholds in duality which religion, society and convention tend to ignore and avoid. The disturbed spaces of conflict, contradiction and chaos become magnetic zones. The imagination seems to have an instinctive trust that while the force of chaos or negativity might wreak havoc on most surfaces, somewhere in its depths the storm has a still centre which longs for fragmentation to come into some form and rhythm. In reference to Beethoven's music, the celebrated pianist Alfred Brendel remarks on the strength and order of its structure: it provides an endurance of form where chaos may shine clear. Thus, form does not annul the chaos; it harnesses its force and opens the possibility of new recognition, participation and integration. Perhaps because such special treasures lie concealed there, the imagination is especially drawn to the worlds of dark possibility. From the seeming wastelands of hate, negativity, despair, loss, chaos and frightening otherness, it can draw forth forms which can begin to transfigure the bleakest anonymity into symbols where affinity might eventually gleam.

The Impossible
Though possibility seems to spring eternal, does it not become redundant when it nears the domain of the impossible? By definition, the impossible suggests the region where possibility cannot preside. Granted there are levels of the impossible which are fixed and resolute. However, much depends on how the impossible is construed, how it is approached and the imaginative and critical quality of the perception which

engages with it. Not everything that seems prima facie impossible is in fact impossible. At least as a minimal requirement, the impossible is open to being questioned and critiqued. There is nothing that cannot be questioned. And often the subversive force of the question begins to reveal that what was considered impossible is not as fixed as was thought heretofore. Some of the greatest discoveries and original pathways to unexpected territories begin to yield themselves when the impossible is approached in the light of a new or neglected question. Frequently, the brightest and most enduring originality begins to emerge when the outer shell of impossibility cracks and a crevice opens into virgin territory no one dreamed was concealed there. Again the oblique and subtle approach of the imagination can re-frame the impossible and draw it towards new engagement and discovery.

The force of the impossible can hold a person prisoner and victim for a whole lifetime. However, in some instances, the impossible can be a call to go beyond. People caught at frontier situations often find hope to go where no one would expect and they can turn something extreme into an experience which brings healing, and liberates new forces of creativity and transformation. This is often the burden and privilege of the prophetic imagination: to see and open pathways of possibility where everyone else accepts that there is but a wasteland. The French poet, Paul Valéry has two wonderful lines which imagine the light that difficulty holds and the intensity of brightness that burns at the heart of of impossibility: *'Une difficulte est une lumière. Une difficulte insurmountable est une soleil.'*

Possibility and Spirit

Possibility is a light sleeper; it can awaken anywhere, at any time, in any form. The permanent valence and passion of possibility suggests an invisible force that enjoys autonomy, imagination and teleology that is not controlled or determined by either the limitations of subjectivity or the frames of space and time. No situation is without possibility. No calendar, clock or geography can control where or how possibility might awaken. The world of possibility owns its own geography of dream. It has its own logic of incipience, prevenience and realisation. Given these characteristics, one is tempted to ask if Spirit might not be another name for possibility? John, the Evangelist, offers a beautifully elemental characterisation of Spirit:

> The wind blows wherever it pleases; you hear its sound, but you cannot tell where it comes from or where it is going.
> This is how it is with all who are born of the Spirit.
> John 3:8-9

This passion and spontaneity are akin to how possibility awakens, disturbs and leads. Spirit suggests a force in which universality and subjectivity are wed. Spirit is the invisible continuum which is also kinetic and transformative. Like spirit, possibility is invisible. It can be disturbing and unpredictable. It is everywhere, has no boundaries or limits. It has infinite patience and can wait a lifetime to be recognised and embraced. As well as the passion, both Spirit and possibility have an absolute precision in how they fit the experience of the individual, coming alive inside the narrative in careful continuity and coherence with its unfolding, even when this may be difficult to discern at the outset. At a meta-level both are ultimately the language of destiny.

If Spirit were another name for possibility, what would that say of Spirit? It would suggest that Spirit is the enemy of monotony and linearity. Spirit would be impatient with whatever is fixed, complacent and narrow. As possibility,

Spirit would want to break through in all situations or individual lives locked in one-dimensionality. It would further indicate that Spirit has an inclusive and telescoped perception which over-views the procession of possibilities on all their various pathways. It would claim that Spirit is the hidden force at the heart of experience which drives it towards cumulative density, or concrescence. Under the sway of Spirit, experience thickens and ripens. Perhaps possibility is indeed the language and grammar of Spirit. Possibility is the natural climate or ferment of those who believe in language as the landscape of emergence where Being articulates itself as Becoming. This is how Spirit speaks: in possibility.

If Spirit is the other name for possibility, what would that say of possibility? It would indicate that possibility is ultimately intimate and personal. It would serve to ground a theory of possibility; no longer could possibility be simply equated with the merely contingent or accidental could-be-ness. Possibility would be seen to have an assurgent source, a sustaining force and a telos of wholeness. Possibility would intend realisation and homecoming that could not be simply gleaned from any single perspective or indeed, from a sum total of perspectives. The horizon of possibility remains forever open. As Spirit, possibility would enjoy a fluent geography where farness and nearness could engage and unite. Finally, not alone would possibility not be limited by the frames of time and space, it would have the force to transform them. As Spirit, possibility would be the agency and arrival place of memory.

Possibility and Death

Time is where possibility becomes manifest. In retrospect, we can see the possibilities that we chose, and perhaps, some of these we did not choose. Similarly, now we can glimpse the outlines of some of the possibilities that surround us. However, we cannot know what the future might bring. From one moment to the next, literally anything can happen. Many of those who awoke this morning stepped into today, into visible continuity with the life they have lived for years; then, this morning something happened, some unexpected news or event suddenly dawned for them, and they will always remember this day as the day that cut their life in two. Now they inhabit a new life and there is no way back to the life they had yesterday. Anything can come. We can never know what is approaching. The future is an unknown land where the caves of the unexpected wait to open, as it approaches us. However, there is one possibility that we already know to be approaching. It is a singular, unique possibility that will arrive regardless of whatever other possibilities may have preceded it, regardless of how dark or creative they might have been. This possibility is so sure that it is even beyond all probability. Indeed, it is more akin to a fact that a possibility. Its name is death.

The possibility of death is certain; it is the permanent possibility that could come alive in any moment, anywhere. Unlike all its sister possibilities, it will not approach in a cluster of invitations or directions. It will come alone, utterly focused. It will not pause or await our desire or readiness. It will not awaken or animate our intention with new prospects or pathways. It is a possibility that will offer us nothing of the future. Unlike all our former possibilities, it will be devoid of any generosity of beginning. This possibility will neither cooperate nor collude with us. It will offer nothing; rather it will take everything. Though it will become manifest in time, it will take time forever from us.

Does the certainty of death as *the* possibility that ends the sequence of life as possibility, not render possibility ultimately empty and negative? What is the purpose of all the invitation and unfolding if all is to end cut off and empty? If possibility were understood only in terms of the visible and the empirical, this could be argued. However, we have tried to ground possibility in the imagination, urgency and secret harvesting of the invisible world. Against such a perspective, death can be viewed as the completion of the invisible harvesting; it is where the visible life finally flows into its invisible source, complete now in its realised form. It is where the visible ceases and where experience is realised in the eternal memory of Spirit. Death is the ultimate translation of the visible into the invisible. It can be viewed as the most transformative possibility of all – the gathering and fulfilment which is no longer vulnerable to the vagaries of loss and limit, the transfiguration and liberation of the self from the segmenting frames of space and time. Life casts off its mortal clothing to become eternal life. The outside becomes absolute and eternal inside. When we die, it becomes possible for us to enter the absolute interior.

Hegel says: 'Death, if that is what we want to call this non-actuality, is of all things the most dreadful, and to hold fast what is dead requires the greatest strength. Lacking strength, Beauty hates the Understanding for asking of her what it cannot do. But the life of the Spirit is not the life that shrinks from death and keeps itself untouched by devastation, but rather the life that endures it and maintains itself in it. It wins its truth only when, in utter dismemberment, it finds itself. It is this power, not as something positive, which closes its eyes to the negative, as when we say of something that it is nothing or is false, and then, having done with it, turn away and pass on to something else; on the contrary, Spirit is this power only by looking the negative in the face, and tarrying with it. This tarrying with the negative is that magical power that converts it into being.'

Resurrection and Possibility

Perhaps against this perspective, it becomes possible to understand the Christian idea of the Resurrection in a new way. Most theologies of the Resurrection become fixated on the questions of the empty tomb or the nexus between history and eternal time. To understand the Resurrection in terms of possibility offers a new perspective which coheres with the desire of experience and the urgency and invitation of possibility in the unfolding and realisation of the individual biographical narrative. The physical arrival of death is but the logical conclusion of the ghosting industry of transience. Resurrection as the death of death means that transience does not have the last word. Resurrection grounds memory as the harvesting of former possibility and the opening and enabling of eternal possibility; now the self is eternal and eternalising. Because death marks the ultimate boundary, the death of death frees the ultimate possibility; the transfiguration of death brings possibility absolutely alive. Resurrection makes of the grave the ultimate cradle.

In breaking through to eternal time, the Resurrection is a breakthrough of giveness so overwhelming and fecund that it engenders possibility at the ontological level. This alteration has occurred at a level deeper than the social, factual or the psychological layers of consciousness. Indeed, this pre-given possibility only becomes available to consciousness the nearer consciousness draws to the limit of its own finite time-line and capacity. Then the depth of this new (not constructed) giveness begins to emerge. It is a giveness that must be received in order for its potency to become active. The future as Resurrection grounds both the past and present. Now possibility instead of constantly engaging with fixed giveness in order to reveal and release new potency is now itself offered as the fruit of an assurgent and passionate giveness. The veil of experience is lifted. Everything can become pure source!

* This text is an altered version of the inaugural lecture in the series, *Platonism and the World Crisis*, delivered in Trinity College in Prof. John Dillon's Centre for the Study of the Platonic Tradition on 20 January 2005.

Notes

1. Cf: Roberto Calasso, *The Marriage of Cadmus and Harmony*, p.99
2. Hans-Georg Gadamer, *The Beginning of Philosophy*, p.17
3. Ibid
4. Bernard Lonergan, *Insight*, p.446.
5. Ibid, p.450.
6. G.W.F. Hegel, *The Phenomenology of Spirit*, p.17.
7. Ibid, p.27.
8. Ibid, p.19.

Bibliography

Roberto Calasso, *The Marriage of Cadmus and Harmony*, NY, 1993.

Hans-Georg Gadamer, *The Beginning of Philosophy*, NY, 1998.

Boris Groys, *Uber das Neue, Versuch einer Kulturokonomie*, Ffm, 1992.

G. W. F. Hegel, *The Phenomenology of Spirit*, transl. by A.V. Miller, Oxford, 1979.

Handbuch philophischer Grundbegriffe, hrsg von Hermann Krings, Hans Michael Baumgartner und Christoph Wild, Munchen,1973

Historisches Worterbuch der Philosophie, Band 6. Wissenschaftliche Buchgesellschaft, Darmstadt, 1984.

Bernard Lonergan, *Insight*, London, NY, 1957.

THE CLOTHING

John O'Donohue

There is something still
Not satisfied
Even after the delicious wait
For nakedness
Has been rewarded with a view
That shimmers
Like a breeze through a meadow
Of flowers
Something that still longs
To travel further
And come to glimpse itself
In the mirror
That hangs in the far hut
Of the heart
These days I find myself
Again and again
With imaginings
Perhaps to keep you true

To the distance
Of the stranger I always hoped
Would come
To take me like the tide at evening
Takes each crevice
From the reach of gutted shore
Into one blue realm
Of fluency whose embrace fulfils.

GOD IS UNFAIR, THANK GOD

Peter McVerry

Peter McVerry is another figure, like Sr Stan, who has brought the issues of poverty, inequality and homelessness to the forefront of Irish public debate. In this article he addresses these issues, but through a particular lens, namely that Christianity must have a domino effect: religious adherence must translate into practical action to improve people's quality of life, particularly those who are on the margins.

Religion Teacher:

Consider the following story:

> Peter is forty years of age. He is an alcoholic. Frequently he drinks his dole money and leaves his wife and two children without any money for food or bills. He sometimes beats her up when he is drunk. He is unfaithful to her and sleeps with any woman he can get. His children fear him, as he hits them if they disobey him. Now Peter did not have a deprived childhood. He grew up in a loving family and went to a fee-paying school. His parents did everything they could for him, but he just rejected all their efforts. He always seemed to care only for himself.

Jim is also forty years old. He too has a wife and two children. He works very hard to support them, often leaving home early and returning late. He has made huge sacrifices over the years to ensure that his children could get a good education. He takes them out every weekend to watch their favourite football team. He lives for his family and would do anything to help them. He goes to Mass every Sunday and insists that his children do the same. They pray together as a family every night before going to bed.

Now Peter and Jim both die and go to the gates of heaven.

What do you think God will do?
a. Jim will be welcomed into the Kingdom of God; Peter will be condemned and excluded from the Kingdom.
b. Both Jim and Peter will be welcomed into the Kingdom of God.
c. Jim will go straight into the Kingdom of God; Peter will get in eventually, but he will have to be punished in purgatory for a long time before he would be allowed in.

Before reading on, tick one of the above for yourself!

Student 1:
'I think God will do (a). Well, it's obvious, isn't it? Peter will be punished by God for doing wrong and Jim will be rewarded for his efforts. Peter didn't care about anyone except himself, he hurt his wife and children, he just wanted to get sloshed and have a good time. But Jim led a good life and cared for his family. He behaved like God wanted him to behave. If God didn't reward Jim and punish Peter, it would

be very unfair of God. Irresponsible of God, in fact. Everyone needs to be held accountable for their actions and if Peter chooses to behave in that way, then he has to take the consequences. I mean, if he had a deprived childhood, or got battered by his dad every night, then there might be some excuse for him. But he didn't. So you couldn't just let him off the hook, as if what he did didn't matter. Of course it mattered, it mattered to his wife and kids who went through hell. He has to be punished for that.'

Student 2:

'I agree with you. I think it's a very stupid question really because the answer is obvious – it has to be (a). I mean could you imagine if Peter was invited into the Kingdom by God, even after a long time in purgatory. Sure, who would bother trying to live a good life, if that was the case? If the likes of him were to be rewarded by God, what would be the point in making sacrifices and making life hard for yourself? Jim would be shown up to be an eejit, doing what he did, putting himself out and caring for others.'

Student 3:

'Well, maybe (c) is a possibility. Of course I agree with you that Peter must be punished. But maybe if he got punished enough, he might come to see how wrong he was and he might be sorry for what he did. Perhaps we shouldn't write him off entirely. Of course punishing him might only make him worse, and then there would be no possibility of him being forgiven. But perhaps God gives everyone another chance, even after death.'

Teacher:
'Hands up all those who think (b) is the right answer.' Only one hand goes up.

I think that hand belongs to God.

Why do I think that that hand belongs to God?

The following is a true story:

> A mother once came to me and said: 'Father, I don't know what to do with my son. He's been on drugs for the past five years. He has robbed everything in my house, the TV, the video, all my jewellery. Sometimes, when he needs his drugs he asks me for money and if I don't give it to him, he might smash the windows in the house. He has even hit me a few times, when I wouldn't give him money. What can I do?' 'And where is he now?' I asked. 'He's in prison, Father, doing five years, and it's the first bit of peace I've had in a long time.' 'And do you go up to visit him?' I enquired. 'Father, every Saturday I go up to see him. Sure, isn't he still my son?'

Gordon Wilson lost his daughter in an IRA bombing in Enniskillen. Several days later, he publicly stated on television that he forgave those who had committed this offence against him. Those who killed his daughter had not repented, indeed they would probably have done the same again if the opportunity had occurred. Forgiving them did not bring his daugher back, nor did it take away the pain of loss that he felt and that he would continue to feel for the rest of his life. But forgiving them removed his desire to punish them. Most of us felt very humbled by the extraordinary response of Gordon Wilson. If he whom God created could forgive those who had so hurt him, then can not the God who created him do likewise?

The life and death of Jesus

We Christians are children of the Resurrection. If Jesus has not risen, then we are the most foolish of all human beings, gullible, deluded and misled. But to understand the Resurrection, we have to understand the death of Jesus. Why was Jesus put to death? Having been brought up in the Hollywood era, we tend to see things in black and white. The film has good guys and bad guys. They fight, but the good guys always win. Jesus was the good guy and although he appeared to have been defeated, he wins at the end by rising from the dead. The Jewish authorities, then, who orchestrated his death must be the bad guys. But Jesus was not put to death by a first-century Saddam Hussein. Jesus was put to death by good people, who led good lives and who thought that by putting Jesus to death, they were doing the right thing, doing what God would have wanted them to do. The Jewish leaders were people of quite extraordinary commitment to their faith and to their God, whose whole lives were lived in obedience to the law of God, as they understood it, and who lived lives of sacrifice, compassion and love. Why did such committed people put Jesus to death? What had Jesus done or said that, to them, merited his death?

The Jewish image of God

For the Jewish faith, *God was a God of the Law*. Faith in God, and allegience to God, was expressed in the exact, meticulous observance of the Law. When God made the covenant with the

Jewish people, God promised to protect them, be with them always and lead them into the promised land. In return, the people of God were to observe the law that God was giving them through Moses. That Law was spelt out and applied to the differing circumstances of life through the teaching of the Rabbis over the centuries. While the purpose of the Law was to teach people how to relate to God and how to relate to each other in compassion, observance of that Law (which had developed into thousands of detailed regulations governing everyday life) was the obligation of every Jew under the covenant and it was the test of their faith and fidelity in God. *To find God, to find salvation in the Kingdom of God, depended on observing the Law of God.* Those who neglected the law, those who derided the law, or those who encouraged people to break the law were unbelievers, a threat to the faith and very existence of the Jewish people, and would obviously, they believed, be excluded by God from the Kingdom.

Now Jesus, as a good Jew, obeyed the law and encouraged people to support the Law. But he proclaimed a higher value than the Law. That higher value was the demands of compassion. If the Jewish faith proclaimed a *God-whose-passion-is-observance-of-the-Law*, Jesus procaimed a *God-whose-passion-is-compassion*.

The demands of compassion involved sometimes breaking the Law:

> Jesus entered the synagogue, and a man was there who had a withered hand. They watched him to see whether he would cure him on the sabbath, so that they might accuse him. And he said to the man who had the withered hand, 'Come forward.' Then he said to them, 'Is it lawful to do good or to do harm on the sabbath, to

save life or to kill?' But they were silent. He looked around at them with anger; he was grieved at their hardness of heart and said to the man, 'Stretch out your hand.' He stretched it out, and his hand was restored. The Pharisees went out and immediately conspired with the Herodians against him, how to destroy him.

Mark 3 v 1-6

Jesus proclaimed a God who could not be found through observance of the Law, but only through compassion:

When the Son of Man comes in his glory, and all the angels with him, then he will sit on the throne of his glory. All the nations will be gathered before him, and he will separate people one from another as a shepherd separates the sheep from the goats, and he will put the sheep at his right hand and the goats at the left. Then the king will say to those at his right hand, 'Come, you that are blessed by my Father, inherit the kingdom prepared for you from the foundation of the world; for I was hungry and you gave me food, I was thirsty and you gave me something to drink, I was a stranger and you welcomed me, I was naked and you gave me clothing, I was sick and you took care of me, I was in prison and you visited me. Then he will say to those at his left hand, 'You that are accursed, depart from me into the eternal fire prepared for the devil and his angels; for I was hungry and you gave me no food, I was thirsty and you gave me nothing to drink, I was a stranger and you did not welcome me, naked and you did not give me clothing, sick and in prison and you did not visit me.'

Matt 25 v 31–46

I try to imagine the reaction of the Jewish authorities to the following story, which is about how to enter the Kingdom of God:

Just then a lawyer stood up to test Jesus. 'Teacher,' he said, 'What must I do to inherit eternal life?' He said to him, 'What is written in the law? What do you read there?' He answered, 'You shall love the Lord your God with all your heart, and with all your soul, and with all your strength, and with all your mind; and your neighbour as yourself.' And he said to him, 'You have given the right answer; do this, and you will live.'

But wanting to justify himself, he asked Jesus, 'And who is my neighbour?' Jesus replied, 'A man was going down from Jerusalem to Jericho, and fell into the hands of robbers, who stripped him, beat him, and went away, leaving him half dead. Now by chance a Priest was going down that road; and when he saw him, he passed by on the other side. So likewise a Levite, when he came to the place and saw him, passed by on the other side. But a Samaritan while travelling came near him; and when he saw him, he was moved with pity. He went to him and bandaged his wounds, having poured oil and wine on them. Then he put him on his own animal, brought him to an inn, and took care of him. The next day he took out two denarii, gave them to the innkeeper, and said, 'Take care of him; and when I come back, I will repay you whatever more you spend.' Which of these three, do you think, was a neighbour to the man who fell into the hands of the robbers?' He said, 'The one who showed him mercy.' Jesus said to him, 'Go and do likewise.'

Luke 10 v 2 5-37

I imagine that the Jewish authorities must have been shocked, furious and highly indignant. In answer to the question: 'What must I do to inherit eternal life?' (to which a good Jew would have replied: 'observe the Law') Jesus tells his Jewish listeners that those (The Priest and the Levite) who prided themselves on their observance of the Law did not, in fact, inherit eternal life, because they had failed in compassion. The one who found eternal life was a person who did not observe the Law (a Samaritan), an unbeliever no less, a person who didn't even believe in the God who gave the Law through Moses.

It was clear to some of the Jewish authorities that Jesus threatened the very basis of their faith. He was undermining the faith of the people in the true God (the God-whose-passion-is-the-observance-of-the-Law) and inventing a different God (the God-whose-passion-is-compassion). He was therefore not only seen as an enemy of the Jewish faith and nation, he was an enemy of the true God, an ally of Satan:

> Then they brought to him a demoniac who was blind and mute; and he cured him, so that the one who had been mute could speak and see. All the crowds were amazed and said, 'Can this be the Son of David?' But when the Pharisees heard it, they said, 'It is only by Beelzebul, the ruler of the demons, that this fellow casts out the demons.'
>
> Matt 12 v 22-24

The clash between the God-whose-passion-is-the-observance-of-the-Law and the God-whose-passion-is-compassion is far from being just a theological debating issue. It affects our whole way of thinking, acting and behaving. The God-whose-passion-is-the-observance-of-the-Law *is a God who judges*, who rewards those who obey and who condemns those who disobey.

Believing in a God of the Law, we know exactly where we stand with God. God is entirely predictable. Insofar as we obey the Law, we are in God's favour, insofar as we disobey the Law we are out of favour with God. Our relationship with God is in our hands, within our control.

But the God-whose-passion-is-compassion *is a God who forgives*. Through forgiveness, God unilaterally restores the relationship with Him that we have broken. God is entirely unpredictable. Our relationship with God is in God's hands.

The difference is well illustrated in the following story:

> After this Jesus went out and saw a tax collector named Levi, sitting at the tax booth; and he said to him, 'Follow me.' And he got up, left everything, and followed him. Then Levi gave a great banquet for him in his house; and there was a large crowd of tax collectors and others sitting at the table with them. The Pharisees and their scribes were complaining to his disciples, saying, 'Why do you eat and drink with tax collectors and sinners?' Jesus answered, 'Those who are well have no need of a physician, but those who are sick; I have come to call not the righteous but sinners to repentance.'
>
> Luke 5 v 27-32

To those who believed in the God-whose-passion-is-the-observance-of-the-Law, it was inconceivable that Jesus would welcome the tax collector. It was a source of scandal. God, they believed, would have nothing but condemnation for such a rogue. Therefore a religious person, who sought to do God's will, would also, they believed, have nothing but condemnation for him. Jesus' invitation to the tax collector proved, to some of the Jewish authorities, that Jesus had nothing but contempt for God and for God's law. Clearly it was God's will, they thought, that he should be got rid of, and as quickly as possible, before he undermined any further people's faith in the true God.

Jesus' treatment of prostitutes probably confirmed their opinion:

> One of the Pharisees asked Jesus to eat with him, and he went into the Pharisee's house and took his place at the table. And a woman in the city, who was a sinner, having learned that he was eating in the Pharisee's house, brought an alabaster jar of ointment. She stood behind him at his feet, weeping, and began to bathe his feet with her tears and to dry them with her hair. Then she continued kissing his feet and anointing them with the ointment. Now when the Pharisee who had invited him saw it, he said to himself, 'If this man were a prophet, he would have known who and what kind of woman this is who is touching him – that she is a sinner.' Jesus spoke up and said to him, 'Simon, I have something to say to you.' 'Teacher,' he replied, 'Speak.' 'A certain creditor had two debtors; one owed five hundred denarii, and the other fifty. When they could not pay, he cancelled the debts for both of them. Now which of them will love him more?' Simon answered, 'I suppose the one for whom he cancelled the greater debt.' And Jesus said to him, 'You have judged rightly.' Then turning toward the woman, he said to Simon, 'Do you see this woman? I entered your house; you gave me no water for my feet, but she has bathed my feet with her tears and dried them with her hair. You gave me no kiss, but from the time I came in she has not stopped kissing my feet. You did not anoint my

head with oil, but she has anointed my feet with ointment. Therefore, I tell you, her sins, which were many, have been forgiven; hence she has shown great love. But the one to whom little is forgiven, loves little.'

Luke 7 v 36-47

Not only did Jesus defend the sinner, but he turned the tables on the Pharisee and declared that by her love, she (who did not obey the Law) was actually closer to God than the one who condemned her (who did obey the Law). Those who were despised and pushed to the margins of society by the just were those who found a welcome from God. The God that Jesus proclaimed, the God-whose-passion-is-compassion, is entirely unpredictable.

And his treatment of the woman taken in adultery may just have been the last straw for some Pharisees!

Jesus went to the Mount of Olives. Early in the morning he came again to the temple. All the people came to him and he sat down and began to teach them. The scribes and the Pharisees brought a woman who had been caught in adultery; and making her stand before all of them, they said to him, 'Teacher, this woman was caught in the very act of committing adultery. Now in the law Moses commanded us to stone such women. Now what do you say?' They said this to test him, so that they might have some charge to bring against him. Jesus bent down and wrote with his finger on the ground. When they kept on questioning him, he straightened up and said to them, 'Let anyone among you who is without sin be the first to throw a stone at her.' And once again he bent down and wrote on the ground. When they heard it, they went away, one by one, beginning with the elders; and Jesus was left alone with the woman standing before him. Jesus straightened up and said to her, 'Woman, where are they? Has no one condemned you?' She said, 'No one, sir.' And Jesus said, 'Neither do I condemn you. Go your way, and from now on do not sin again.'

John 8 v 1-11

The Unfair God

The God-whose-passion-is-compassion is totally unfair and most of us actually resent it. In the story earlier, I think that the first reaction of many of us is to think that a God who could forgive Peter was totally unfair to Jim, even perhaps unjust. We resent God forgiving Peter. We resent God being compassion:

> For the kingdom of heaven is like a landowner who went out early in the morning to hire labourers for his vineyard. After agreeing with the labourers for the usual daily wage, he sent them into his vineyard. When he went out about nine o'clock, he saw others standing idle in the marketplace; and he said to them, 'You also go into the vineyard, and I will pay you whatever is right.' So they went. When he went out again about noon and about three o'clock, he did the same. And about five o'clock he went out and found others standing around; and he said to them, 'Why are you standing here idle all day?' They said to him, 'Because no one has hired us.' He said to them, 'You also go into the vineyard.' When evening came, the owner of the

vineyard said to his manager, 'Call the labourers and give them their pay, beginning with the last and then going to the first.' When those hired about five o'clock came, each of them received the usual daily wage. Now when the first came they thought they would receive more; but each of them also received the usual daily wage. And when they received it, they grumbled against the landowner, saying, 'These last worked only one hour, and you have made them equal to us who have borne the burden of the day and the scorching heat.' But he replied to one of them, 'Friend, I am doing you no wrong; did you not agree with me for the usual daily wage? Take what belongs to you and go; I choose to give to this last the same as I give to you. Am I not allowed to do what I choose with what belongs to me? Or are you envious because I am generous?' So the last will be first, and the first will be last.'

Matt 20 v 1-16

Most of us expect God to be fair, to reward us for the sacrifices and effort which we, like Jim, have made, and to punish those who, like Peter above, live selfish and uncaring lives. We want God to be a God of the Law. Like the labourers in the story above, we actually resent a God-whose-passion-is-compassion, for such a God is essentially unfair.

The famous story of the prodigal son is the story of two Gods, a God of the Law and a God of compassion. The younger son, who knows himself to be a sinner, is entirely dependent on the father being a father of compassion. He returns to throw himself on the father's compassion. If the father were to be predictable, and therefore fair, he ought to punish his younger son for his ingratitude and reward his elder son for his faithfulness. The elder brother does not want his father to be compassionate, he wants him to be fair. But to his surprise, the father is totally unpredictable and treats the sinner even better than he treated the just brother! The just brother resents his father's compassion.

> Then Jesus said, 'There was a man who had two sons. The younger of them said to his father, "Father, give me the share of the property that will belong to me." So he divided his property between them. A few days later the younger son gathered all he had and travelled to a distant country, and there he squandered his property in dissolute living. When he had spent everything, a severe famine took place throughout that country, and he began to be in need. So he went and hired himself out to one of the citizens of that country, who sent him to his fields to feed the pigs. He would gladly have filled himself with the pods that the pigs were eating; and no one gave him anything. But when he came to himself he said, "How many of my father's hired hands have bread enough and to spare, but here I am dying of hunger! I will get up and go to my father, and I will say to him, 'Father, I have sinned against heaven and before you; I am no longer worthy to be called your son; treat me like one of your hired hands'." So he set off and went to his father. But while he was still far off, his father saw him and was filled with compassion; he ran and put his arms around him and kissed him. Then the son said to him, "Father, I have sinned against heaven and before you; I am no longer worthy to be called your son." But the father said to his slaves, "Quickly, bring out a robe – the best one – and put it on him; put a ring on his finger and sandals on his feet. And get the fatted calf and kill it, and let us eat and celebrate; for this son of mine was dead and is alive again; he was lost and is found!" And they began to celebrate.

'Now his elder son was in the field; and when he came and approached the house, he heard music and dancing. He called one of the slaves and asked what was going on. He replied, "Your brother has come, and your father has killed the fatted calf, because he has got him back safe and sound." Then he became angry and refused to go in. His father came out and began to plead with him. But he answered his father, "Listen! For all these years I have been working like a slave for you, and I have never disobeyed your command; yet you have never given me even a young goat so that I might celebrate with my friends. But when this son of yours came back, who has devoured your property with prostitutes, you killed the fatted calf for him!" Then the father said to him, "Son, you are always with me, and all that is mine is yours. But we had to celebrate and rejoice, because this brother of yours was dead and has come to life; he was lost and has been found."'

Luke 15 v 11-32

Those who truly welcome a God-whose-passion-is-compassion are those for whom a God-whose-passion-is-observance-of-the-Law would bring only condemnation, namely sinners, and those who know themselves to be poor in the sight of God. They cannot rely on their good works to save them, for they have none, they depend on God's compassion. To them, the God that Jesus revealed was, indeed, good news, for it opened the gates of heaven to them. Those gates had been firmly closed to them by the God-whose-passion-is-observance-of-the-Law:

The Spirit of the Lord is upon me, because he has anointed me to bring good news to the poor.

Luke 4 v 18

To those who asked how could they recognise God when God would be revealed, Jesus declared himself to be the revelation of God, and the evidence he offered was his own compassion. The God-whose-passion-is-compassion was revealed in him:

> John summoned two of his disciples and sent them to the Lord to ask, 'Are you the one who is to come, or are we to wait for another?' Jesus had just then cured many people of diseases, plagues, and evil spirits, and had given sight to many who were blind. And he answered them, 'Go and tell John what you have seen and heard: the blind receive their sight, the lame walk, the lepers are cleansed, the deaf hear, the dead are raised, the poor have good news brought to them.'
>
> John 7 v 18-22

Hence, Jesus was welcomed enthusiastically by many who were poor and by many tax collectors and sinners, but rejected by many who were righteous. The God that Jesus revealed was good news to the poor, but bad news for the righteous, who instead of getting some reward from God for their efforts, saw sinners getting the same treatment – sometimes even better treatment – from God as themselves.

Jesus was put to death by good people, acting for good reasons, because the God that Jesus revealed had radical consequences for the ordering, behaviour and structures of society, consequences which threatened the existing order of society. Those who put Jesus to death believed, according to their image of God, that they were acting in accordance with the will of God.

People-whose-passion-is-compassion

The followers of Jesus, then, are people-whose-passion-is-compassion. The values, attitudes and behaviour of people-whose-passion-is-compassion are radically transformed by their belief. It challenges their selfishness, their prejudices and their desires and dreams. To believe in a God who forgives the offender compels them to forgive those who have hurt them, not seven times, but seventy times seven times. To believe in a God who reaches out to those whom society disregards or despises compels them to reach out to those on the margins, in support and welcome. They are prepared to lay down reputation, riches, property, even life itself, for those in need.

People-whose-passion-is-compassion seek to build a society whose economic, social and political structures and policies are shaped by a radical concern for those in need. To believe in a God who has a passionate concern for those on the margins compels us to struggle to create a society which has a passionate concern for those on the margins. To believe in a God who does not condemn compels us to struggle to create a society which does not condemn.

People-whose-passion-is-compassion are unwilling to restrict their faith to merely individual, personal moral choices. Theirs is a radical faith, which challenges those in power and those who support them at the ballot box.

The Resurrection of Jesus was God's confirmation that the God-whose-passion-is-compassion, whom Jesus revealed in his own deeds and words, is indeed, the true God. Those whose-passion-is-compassion are today the revelation of that God.

UPDATE

Micheal O'Siadhail

Micheal O'Siadhail's brand new poem 'Update', written especially for this book, reminds us of the urgency of making a practical response to the marginalised.

Given a globe of flash and breaking news
Where swarms of flies on a starving face
Crawl a screen of glass
Between comfort and hunger, refuse

To fade when zapped but leave a creeping trace
Within a psyche's magic lantern,
An afterimage of concern,
Given a globe has watched the wasting face

We can no longer say we didn't know.
Gone the slow dispatch our alibi
For hindsight, each plea
Immediate and doubled in its nag and echo

Haunts the ear of every brother's keeper.
Bulletin by bulletin, update by update,

Famine's balance sheet.
Bitter wind-sower, whirlwind reaper

Still so world-foolish and pennywise,
Children's children know we know.
Tomorrow, tomorrow, tomorrow.
Abel's child now starves before our eyes.

A NECESSARY PASSION

Raphael Gallagher CSsR

In post 'Celtic Tiger' Ireland all the old absolutes and certainties have melted away. These themes are reflected in the work of our creative artists, from the writings of John McGahern to the music of U2. In such circumstances articulating a prescription or blueprint for a solution to our problems is problematic. Raphael Gallagher's starting point is that we are at an in-between time in history in Ireland, caught between a rich tradition and an as yet unformed new direction. As the old tree of established structures is dying it is not easy to graft anew to the future vine. This transition brings a plethora of questions and challenges many of our traditionally cherished values.

We are all in favour of it, but justice can be such an abstract idea that it says very little about what we really want to do. We are moved to action, not by justice, but by a perception that an injustice is being done. Many of us do not get that far, protected as we are by our comfort zones. The result is that a vague idea of happiness is taking root as the guiding principle for social living in Ireland. When I am unhappy (and I decide what happiness is) then my first instinct is to seek my own happiness, and the devil take the hindmost. If most people are generally happy, and I have read that Ireland has been recently judged top of the league in terms of quality of life, it is little wonder that a passion for the plight of others is at a low ebb. If I am happy, and others are not, it is their fault. They are whiners and begrudgers. The move from a sense of justice, even if abstract, through a passion for injustice to a generalised sense of creating a 'happy Ireland' is a disturbing trend. Its genealogy is worth tracing.

Traditional Ireland, for example the years in which Sister Stan grew up, did have a sense of justice. Granted that the idea may have been abstract, justice was surely administered. How it was administered is the first genealogical root. Two broad groups can be identified: the System Protectors and the Citizen Protectors. The System Protectors tended to argue, 'Look, I am not certain that this person is a recidivist robber or a madman or a member of a terrorist organisation, but it is better not to take any chances because the danger to the System is too great'. The Citizen Protectors would have argued, 'Excuse me, there can be no practical justice if a person is kept locked away when there is no credible evidence that they are a continuing danger to society'. The System Protectors were in control in those years, both in Church and State. Irish prisons, asylums and reformatories probably had many people in them who should never have been there. The protesting voices were few and easily quelled.

Why was this so? The usual suspects include political conservatism, judicial caution and collusion between the powers that be in Church and State. One remote genealogical line of all three is rarely commented on. I believe it is to be found in a particular presentation of religion that was in the Ireland of those years, most obviously in the Catholic Church.

A Perfect Society

The Ireland of Sister Stan's youth was partly formed by a view of the Catholic Church that had its origins in the First Vatican Council (1869-70). The Church was presented as the true, perfect, spiritual and supernatural society. So perfect, indeed, in itself that it was superior to any other form of society. The Church was a spiritual society, entirely of the supernatural order, and every other form (including that of the Irish State) was inferior by its very nature. Of course the Church had to accept that there were Catholic sinners, but their sinning was explained in terms of how they had become infected by the wicked inferior world outside the Church. It was not the Church's fault if there were sinners: this is the view re-iterated by Pope Pius XII in his encyclical letter *Of the Mystical Body* (1943): 'it cannot be laid to her (i.e. the Church's charge) if some of her members fall weak or wounded'.

The Church surely cared about Irish society, but the logic of the caring was determined by the view the Church had of itself. The problems of Ireland could be solved if, ideally, all returned to the true Catholic Church, which offered the perfect society in which to be saved. Failing this, the problems of Irish society were viewed as objects of the charity of the Church. This was commendable, and I have no doubt about the benefits many received from the caring Church organisations of those years.

It is the logic behind the caring that interests me. The Church, a perfect society that had within itself all the means necessary for the good life, offered its charity to those in need. This meant that the question of injustice in society did not present itself as an issue of direct concern. It would be unfair to insinuate that Church people of those years were not caring: the Society of St Vincent de Paul and various Confraternities are only some examples of the caring. When the sense of caring is driven by the charity of a perfect supernatural Church it is not unfair to say that this obscured the analysis of the deeper roots of injustice.

A Perfect World?

A more recent genealogical line can be traced to the impact of the Second Vatican Council. In one of its more important Constitutions, *The Church in the Modern World*, we are told that the Church has something to learn from the world. 'The Church profits from the experience of past ages, from the progress of the sciences, and from the riches hidden in various cultures, through which greater light is shed on human nature and new avenues of truth are opened up' (Paragraph 44). This gave an impetus for a new vision, and it is plainly difficult to graft onto the view that a perfect Church had nothing to learn from an imperfect world.

Though the Council itself is cautious on the independence of the world in relation to the Church, the impact of this new vision had a deep effect on Irish society and its view of justice. If in the first genealogical root the dominant view was of a Church that treated the world as very definitely unequal and inferior, in this second root there is the beginning of a view that society did not need the Church. Some went as far as to say that the Church was only a hindrance to the progress of society. Authors like Marcel Gauchet were quoted: his thesis is that religion is a phenomenon tied to a particular phase of human history which, happily so in his view, has been superseded. The death of God was announced, and post-Catholic Ireland proclaimed.

This was to have consequences for the work of justice. The 1970s in Ireland were marked by serious efforts to create a Church that regarded the commitment to justice as an integral part of its work of preaching: 'a faith that does justice' was the inspiring call to action. This newly planted root got substance from the commitment of many people, notably some religious congregations who took the challenge to heart. Sister Stan can be seen as a key figure in this generation of committed Catholics who decisively rejected the genealogical line of the First Vatican Council and worked for a Church faithful to the Second Vatican Council in its commitment to justice issues. Charity alone no longer sufficed, nor obviously an abstract view of justice. To be real and effective, justice must be concrete and social: individuals must be treated with justice by creating structures in society that guaranteed the delivery of this faith-based justice.

Leaving aside the tensions within Church circles about the need to replace the older genealogical line with a new family of Church people publicly committed to justice, the most challenging point is the growth in Ireland of those who see Irish society, newly liberated from the domination of the Church, as having no need for a Church voice. It is not just a relegation of the Church to a position where it is one voice among others who have a stake in society, such as trade unions or lobby interests. Perhaps the future of Irish society would be healthier, in the sense of happier, without a public Church interference in the affairs of society. If someone wants to be a Catholic, that is a private choice with no public bearing. A wheel came full circle, and the shock waves of various scandals only hastened what was already happening. It was no longer the Church that was regarded as perfect, quite the opposite. The institutions of society were seen as more truthful, and they could expose injustices better than any Church institution. I have not actually seen anyone intelligently argue that a perfect Irish society would be one totally free of the Church, but there is an undeniable sense of a rejection of the older perfect Church with its now too obvious feet of clay.

The genealogy of the two traditions of justice in contemporary Ireland goes some way towards explaining why there is a clash of interpretations about 'what is best for Irish society'. It is this impasse that has led many to adopt the notion that what we really want in Ireland is a society of vaguely happy people. The aspiration for a just society has been replaced by the dream of happy people loosely connected in different settings. The Church can have a role if it provides therapy for people in their search for personal happiness, but little else is to be expected from or allowed to the Church in the public forum.

Future Perfect?
Contemporary Ireland is not uncaring. But is the rationale for our caring sufficient to sustain the bonds that are necessary for a practical justice that is structurally cohesive? On this point too, I want to explore the genealogical roots of recent competing visions of Irish society.

Benevolence, a general sense of goodwill, is often presented as the best family line to pursue. An eloquent contemporary exponent of this view is the philosopher Peter Singer who argues 'if it is in our power to prevent something bad from happening, without thereby sacrificing anything of comparable moral importance, we ought morally to do so'. Strong as the argument is on a utilitarian level, I believe it places the burden of justice in the wrong place. The problem of injustice should be tackled not merely because it happens to be part of the overall good that we can achieve in society, and which would be overlooked were we to stand idly by. The reason why there is a moral duty to be involved in the struggle for justice is because it is *individual people* who are not treated accordingly as fellow humans. The passion for justice comes from the cry of people who are obviously treated unjustly. It is never some abstract principle in my head, no matter how high-minded, that fuels this passion.

A more convincing genealogical line is that associated with the elimination of injustice by an appeal to human rights. If a person has a right to be treated with justice, then we surely have a duty to see that justice is done in terms of rights being accorded to people. This is very appealing as a basis, but there is a difficulty. The dominating view of human rights, in the slipstream of the UN Declaration of 1948, has stressed the rights of individuals. Little progress, in the Western world at least, has been made on economic, social and political rights. With regard to a passion for justice this is a crucial point. Theories of human rights that do not adequately address the structural problem of injustice, and the need for a far-sighted redistribution of resources, will only go so far. Some progress has been made on solving this difficulty, most notably by philosophers like John Rawls. In his seminal *A Theory of Justice* (1971) he envisages society as a rational scheme of cooperation between individuals who all agree to the distribution of benefits and burdens. He envisages a type of contract that includes a commitment to equal liberty for all and a guarantee that the maximum benefits to be given to the minimum members of society. His argument, in essence, is that with such a view of society the least well off will be better off than in any other type of arrangement. It is crucial that we support the movement towards human rights as part of our passion for justice, and the Catholic Church is a latecomer on the scene in this regard. However, I am concerned that the view of human rights that is beginning to become dominant, as is obvious from debates about the proposed new European Union Constitution, is not sufficiently social in character to give a moral basis for justice. Even in Rawls' very appealing theory, the argument rests in the last analysis on self-interest. It is in my interest to ensure that those on the margins, the minimum of society in Rawls' view, be treated justly because one day I might find myself in that same position and I would surely hope that society would look after *me*. The problem is not with human rights, in themselves. About these we have no choice. The difficulty arises when these are seen only as the rights of individuals. Justice is supremely a social passion. When human rights are seen only as the rights of individuals to the exclusion of social, economic and political rights, the division in societies, like the US, for example, can take very damaging forms.

Future Imperfect
The genealogy of the line of development in Irish society, from an abstract sense of justice through a phase of engaged social Catholics to the acceptance of individual happiness as the ideal, raises the question whether there are alternative blood lines to investigate. One comes to mind, once again in symmetry with the type of Catholic Church hoped for by the Second Vatican Council. In the same Constitution that I quoted above, *The Church in the Modern World,* there is an inviting prospect: we are asked to take into consideration 'some more urgent problems deeply affecting the human race at the present day in the light of the Gospel and of human experience'. It is beyond dispute that injustice should be counted among the more serious problems of the day, and the prospect of returning to the Gospel and to take on board the human experience of those who suffer injustice is appealing because it puts the more recent genealogical roots to a more testing examination.

'For I was hungry and you fed me, I was thirsty and you gave me drink'. This is from verse 35 of the twenty-fifth chapter of the Gospel of Matthew. To explain how this may operate as a more inclusive and solid foundation of action for justice I would draw attention to a number of contrasts in the chapter taken as a whole. The affirmation is particular (*I* was hungry), but the implication is universal. Jesus goes on to say that it is on the basis of this particular affirmation that the general judgment of our lives will be based (verses 44 to 46). The least in this world is judged as the criterion for entry into the Kingdom. I have taken one verse, that relating to the hungry person, but the chapter also mentions the naked, the sick and the prisoner. What is done now (*you fed me*) has long-term implications. Entry into the kingdom is given, or refused, on the basis of what we do for the hungry, naked, or imprisoned person. The individual (you fed *me*) is an implicit test of how we view society in general. The Gospel chapter gives no indication that the distinctions of class, creed or sex have anything to do with the argument. Once *a person* is hungry, that is all that matters. You don't pause for thought and wonder 'is she one of ours?' There is one other interesting contrast in the text. The human, that is the hungry person, is identified with the divine, in that you are feeding the God who is imaged in that person.

It is dangerous to try to prove anything directly by quoting the Scriptures. Let's leave that to the devil. Yet this chapter of Matthew's Gospel is suggestive in its indication of why we should be bothered about injustice in Irish society. The argument undermines, in a radical way, the genealogical lines that can be traced back to the idea of a perfect Church caring for an imperfect world. It broadens the perspective of those genealogical lines that see justice as a matter of procedures, rights and individual interest.

This quotation from Matthew's Gospel is part of a larger fresco of the Last Judgment. Images can instil fear or foster hope. The Last Judgment is often used in the fear-instilling mode. In seeking for the motivation as to why we should be bothered about injustice in Ireland, the image offers a more positive vista. The Kingdom of God is often compared to a banquet. The problem arises as to who will be offered an invitation. By excluding people from the banquet of this life, we are implicitly saying that we do not think them worthy of entry into the Banquet that is the Kingdom of God. That is precisely what we do when we do not take the victims of injustice seriously. We exclude them from society, in various ways. Hunger is the most dramatic form, but there are all sorts of other exclusions implied by poor housing conditions, unequal educational opportunities, and discriminatory rules for political participation. The passion for justice, once again, is seen to begin with a concrete concern for an individual person, but it is rooted most deeply when we see the individual in a social context.

We can see, in view of this, the relevance of the second indication of the search for a better way of articulating the necessary passion for justice: 'in the light of human experience'. A quotation from the encyclical letter of Pope John Paul II *On Social Concern* offers a way into this: 'and there are others – the many who have little or nothing – who do not succeed in realising their basic human vocation because they are deprived of essential human goods'. (Paragraph 28) It is a shivering thought that we might be responsible for depriving others of those goods that are intrinsic to their growth as human beings. One could argue that one is born human, and that each one has the internal resources to realise their full potential. This argument falls down, like earlier ones I mentioned, because it sees the human person as an isolated individual. We are born human, in a certain sense, but we become fully human through the process of participating in social life. If social life is organised in such a way that someone, even one, is deprived of those goods which are necessary for human growth then there is something askew. This, surely, is the experience we can glean from life. The example of hunger is again the most dramatic one: a starving person plainly lacks something essential for life. Much will of course depend on how we define the vocation to be a human person. But it is surely possible to agree on some criteria, other than the obvious one of food. Freedom of speech, access to education, adequate housing, and political participation come to mind. The list is indicative and not exhaustive. Though very sketchy, this does point to how a passion for justice cannot be an optional extra, either on the basis of human experience or in the light of the Gospel.

It is not that there is no such thing as society, as a lady once famously claimed. Society exists, but it is prone to becoming embedded in unjust structures precisely because it is a human creation. These injustices cry out to us, not because they are unjust according to some abstract criterion, but because they are depriving some members of our society from reaching their full human potential. There is no such thing as a perfect society: that is what the lady should have said. Imperfection marks the human condition, and injustice is a fruit of uncorrected imperfections. Perfection will exist only in the Kingdom, but the memory of what Jesus laid down as a criterion for entry into the Kingdom is a credible basis for a social engagement to eliminate personal and structural injustices in our society. The genealogical roots that shaped the Ireland of Sister Stan's generation of Irish people may have obvious fault-lines. To acknowledge is not an exercise in blame laying. It can lead to seeking a better base for the exciting passion for social justice 'in the light of the Gospel and of human experience'.

EASTER PEOPLE

Gordon Linney

The Catholic Church is not alone in producing prophetic figures who are willing to ask awkward questions about the state of Irish society. For many years Archdeacon Gordon Linney has taken on this role in the Church of Ireland and denounced injustice, inequality and the poverty of leadership. In this article he continues his quest for a mutually critical correlation between the world of contemporary experience and the Christian tradition.

Signs of Hope

Some years ago members of the ecumenical Taizé Community from France spent some time in the Dublin area with ecumenical church groups. In preparation for their visit they invited each group to identify signs of hope within their area. These might include charitable or community projects or the caring work of individuals. The intention of the Taizé Brothers was to help people recognise and appreciate that good things are happening all around us, but they are not always known or appreciated. Bad news seems to dominate the headlines and it can be difficult for those who believe in an ultimate goodness to remain hopeful.

Making Sense of our World

In one very troubled part of our world the remarkable life and work of Margaret Hassan was truly a sign of hope. While most people across the world argued about the existence or non-existence of weapons of mass destruction in Iraq she got on with her caring work. Reports of her brutal murder remind us that evil recognises no boundaries and that the greatest of international disputes and conflicts are ultimately personal and local in that they affect families and individuals. Margaret Hassan was the victim of twisted moral disorder.

Events in Iraq and the Middle East have dominated the news for years and in a particular way illustrate the difficulty we often face distinguishing between what is good and what is bad. People are anxious and confused at what has been happening there, but bitterly divided over its merits or otherwise.

Many have been critical of the American/British action and our government's tacit support indicated by its approval of the use of Shannon Airport as a stopover for US military flights. It is said that whilst we may not like this involvement we cannot afford to incur the economic wrath of the United States! Where does the concept of 'goodness' fit into that scenario? It is easy to disguise self-interest as a freedom campaign, but difficult to sustain the deception.

One of the main objections of the opponents of the invasion is that it lacked the sanction of the United Nations, and therefore a moral or legal authority. But here again there are issues. The record of the UN in places such as Rwanda and Serbia/Croatia leaves much to be desired. In these and other places, vested and conflicting interests of major powers prevented an agreed global response to situations and ordinary people suffered and died as a result. Who can forget the shameful abandonment of the people of Srebenica by Dutch

UN troops and the consequential massacre of its men and boys by invading Serbs? What indications were there, are there, that the UN could ever deal effectively with Saddam Hussein's regime and the many atrocities inflicted on masses of his own people and his threat to his neighbours? Indeed there are suggestions that some UN officials were themselves compromised in the oil for food programme.

On the Sunday that I was baptised in September 1939 Britain and France declared war on Germany in defence of Poland following its invasion by Germany. At the end of World War II Poland was abandoned by the Western Allies and left to the mercy of the Soviet Union. Thousands of Free Polish troops who had fought courageously with Britain were sent home to imprisonment and worse under Stalin's regime, a regime that was every bit as ruthless as the Nazis.

These examples show how difficult it can be to make sense of our world or to hope that at the end of the day decisions will be primarily motivated by what is moral and what is just. A long time ago Pontius Pilate got it right, politically but not morally, when he pronounced that it was expedient that one man should die. We live in an imperfect world where too many innocents are victims of political expediency. At the same time one must accept the realities faced by political leaders in making decisions no matter how good their intentions from a moral point of view.

It is said that politics is the art of the possible, but the possibilities are defined by what people and their political masters feel and the values that inform their decision-making. It is arguable that much of the Middle East trouble stems from the deep sense of injustice felt by Palestinian refugees and their feeling that the West is preoccupied with its own economic success and security and has little concern for their problems. In all this confusion where can we find help given the need for politically independent moral voices that are prepared to engage in real debate as to what is good, what is right, what is best? Furthermore those who believe that hope is more than wishful thinking will recognise that hope and morality are close relations.

The Misuse Of Religion
There is little doubt that religion is important to many of the people engaged in these conflict situations but the question has to be asked: Does it help?

A few months ago it was reported that a US army chaplain serving in Iraq, after conducting worship for troops spoke about 'visiting the wrath of God' on the enemy! Not very far away, but on the other side of the same conflict, were people who believe that suicide bombings and other atrocities have the blessing of Allah (the very same God) and that such activities attract special rewards in the next life.

At Drumcree over several years we saw an Irish version of the same thing. Masses of men who had attended a Church of Ireland service nearby surged down the road 'for God and Ulster' to attack the army and the police and anyone else within range with whom they disagreed. On the other side of the barrier it was reported on one occasion that at an open air Mass a priest offered the sign of peace to army personnel on duty but declined an invitation to accept army hospitality in return. How genuine was the peace?

This kind of blinkered theology is deeply rooted in the mind. Its nature is to denounce in others what it is itself. It can lead to actions and judgements resting on prejudices which are elevated to the status of principles which make objective moral judgement much more difficult.

Last November in the US presidential election it is said that President Bush's campaign team focused on groups across America who shared his strong conservative religious views and especially what were described as 'family values'. The subtext was, at least in part, anti-gay, and was a reaction to the campaign for the legalisation of same sex marriage. This, for many Americans, was of far greater concern than the war in Iraq where thousands were being killed and injured, including young American soldiers. Environmental and other issues hardly rated. Perhaps it would be more useful if people could learn to think in terms of 'families valued' rather than 'family values.' We could then focus on the hurt and pain inflicted on many innocent people by varying degrees of religious fanaticism built on an understanding of God that is seriously inadequate to deal with the moral complexities of the modern world.

We need church leaders, prophets, who have the courage to challenge people to broaden their minds and to think deeply about the radical and costly implications of what it means to be a Christian in the modern world. In the Old Testament era the Jews had to meet a similar challenge. They were very conscious of their status as the *chosen* people and went on to assume that this placed them in a position of privilege. Divine Right was on their side and no harm could come their way. (We hear echoes of this today in modern Israel on the land issue and in America where it would appear that almost every political speech ends with the invocation 'God bless America'). But again and again the prophets pointed out to the Jews that they were chosen not for privilege, but for responsibility and that that would be costly. This was a message they did not want to hear.

Making sense of Religion

In the Irish context we see at first hand the misuse and abuse of religion for political reasons that divided this island, sometimes with support from the Churches. Some would even contend that religion is the problem. I would argue from my Northern Ireland experience that in recent times, if not historically, the Churches have been, on balance, an important influence for good with Church leaders playing an important role in shaping the future. Inevitably churchmen with extreme views attracted attention while parish clergy and laity of all denominations who worked quietly and positively, often in an ecumenical way, went unsung and unrecognised. Individuals like the late Senator Gordon Wilson, and there were many like him, who despite terrible personal loss, pleaded for non-retaliation and for peace and had a profound influence for good. It was often the people with most reason to be angry who were most forgiving and conciliatory. The world marvelled and listened with respect and admired the values that they upheld, however painful or costly.

It is much easier to identify moral issues with religious/political undertones in extreme situations such as Northern Ireland where the issue of sectarianism was there for all to see. But issues of social inclusion and economic fairness can be lost sight of especially in the age of spin doctoring which is so prevalent in the Republic of Ireland. Reflecting on the character of Irish life in the age of the Celtic Tiger one would have to enquire about the extent to which religious belief affects the values and lifestyle of people in the South any longer.

Surveys indicate that the vast majority of people are religious in some sense of that word, but to what end?

Traditional religious conformity has been in decline for some years even though at critical times such as the Omagh bombing and the September 11 outrages in the US it was to Church-led events that people turned for help and consolation.

Nonetheless for the Churches credibility is a huge problem. Scandals are an issue, but the problem goes much deeper. Some are clearly anti-Church while others have genuine intellectual difficulties with religious language and concepts that do not fit easily into this age of rapid scientific and technological progress. Does religious faith make sense? Is it believable? Is it relevant to modern self-confident man?

One wonders are the Churches in denial here. Are these questions too painful to contemplate? It is easier to focus on issues of internal discipline and practice rather than engage with and challenge aggressive secularism. During long years of liturgical reform in the Church of Ireland there were those who argued that services in modern language with modern hymns would attract more of the younger generations! But something much more radical than substituting 'you' for 'thou' was and is required.

The answer lies to some extent in making that vital connection between faith and life; that committed Christian people live by what they commend to others. I believe passionately that the values we hold as Christians and often share with other great world religions make sense and are beneficial not only to Christians but to society as a whole. That was clearly evident in the case of Gordon Wilson.

The Essential Gospel

Earlier I referred to the difficulties people have with what they perceive to be outdated religious language and imagery. That is especially true of the person of Jesus. It is possible to establish some level of common mind with many who might not see themselves as religious in a formal way by focusing on the humanity of Jesus.

The life of Jesus is the perfect example of human potential, but too often in the past Jesus has been used to demonstrate how bad we are, whereas his entire ministry pointed in the other direction as he encouraged and helped people to think of who and what they might become.

His attitude included everyone, welcomed everyone, not because they were 'good' but because they were human beings who needed healing, acceptance, self-respect, a sense of personal worth. People have the same needs today and especially those who are on the margins of society. His was an attitude of inclusiveness where diversity was welcomed and not merely tolerated.

Against this background one can recognise the basis on which a wide range of human rights are vindicated; issues of justice, freedom and peace, the right to work and an entitlement to food and shelter. This is the stuff of what St James called 'true religion', something the churches must continue to focus their energies on.

Life Before Death

Easter is a foundational event of the Christian movement. Sometimes Pentecost is described as the birthday of the Church, but Easter is much more important. It has been said that since the first Easter Day when that stone was rolled away from the tomb, stones have moved ever since to build not only churches, cathedrals, and monasteries, but also schools, universities and hospitals. This event in Jerusalem in the first century gave rise to a new world order. Somehow we have lost much of the 'oomph' that we should derive from a better understanding of what Easter is about.

Too often it is presented as a future event – easily dismissed by the cynic as pie in the sky, the kind of religion once famously defined by an English schoolboy as 'believing wot you know ain't true!'

It is no accident that baptism is a central feature of the Easter liturgy with its an emphasis on 'walking with Christ in the newness of his risen life'. In other words it is a contemporary lifestyle as well as a future hope. The Third World relief organisation Christian Aid makes this point with the motto *We Believe In Life Before Death* and from that perspective reaches out to address the needs of the poorest and most vulnerable people on the planet. This in no way devalues the *beyond* dimension of Easter which is central to Christian belief.

A Christian commitment to social justice and the things that affect people's everyday lives is not an optional extra for the super good but a practical expression of how life in all its phases is to be understood. St James in his Epistle wrote:

> Suppose a brother or sister is in rags with not enough food for the day and one of you says, 'good luck to you, keep yourselves warm, and have plenty to eat' but does nothing to supply their bodily needs what is the good of that?
>
> St James 2:15,16

Last autumn the Economist Intelligence Unit (EIU) published a report, which stated that Ireland had the highest quality of life in the world. It omitted to say for whom! Further it claimed that income inequality and educational levels did not have a major bearing on the quality of life and highlighted our material well-being, low unemployment, political liberties and stable family life.

Around the same time President McAleese, in her inauguration day speech, was speaking of our impatience for many frustratingly inadequate things to be better. 'We worry about matters that hollow out our optimism like youth suicide, racism, binge-drinking, street crime and corruption. We know our current economic success cannot be a destination in itself but a route to one of our primary ambitions as a nation – to bring prosperity and security to every single citizen'.

It would be foolish to pretend that Ireland is not a prosperous and successful country in which many, even a majority, of its citizens have an excellent quality of life. But why do politicians and other commentators try to pretend that there are no serious exceptions and that everyone is fine when every statistic tells us the opposite?

The Economic Social and Research Institute has pointed out that we now have the highest level of relative income poverty in Europe, 21 per cent of the population living on less than 60 per cent of the median income of 2001. And the gap is widening. In 1994 2.8 per cent of the population over sixty-five were living on less than half of the median income. By 2001 the figure had risen to 18.2 per cent. In the same period recipients of the widow's pension living in poverty rose from 5.5 per cent to 42.1 per cent and the percentage of children living in relative poverty rose from 9.4 per cent to 14.2 per cent.

Much of this neglect was compounded by a series of swingeing cuts to social services and benefits for some of the most vulnerable in our society introduced within days of the re-election of the present government. How cynical can we be?

In the recent Book of Estimates announced in November by the Minister for Finance €69 million was provided for the Horse and Greyhound Racing Fund: that's €5 million more than what is provided to the National Treatment Purchase Fund and twice the amount provided for adult education initiatives. In this connection it is worth noting that throughout what we call 'the free world' between 50 per cent and 60 per cent of all prison inmates have serious learning disabilities. Money spent on education is money very well spent.

These figures are only samples of a political and economic mindset that is seriously deficient when it comes to good government, which must demonstrate a proper concern for all citizens, and especially those who are vulnerable through age or disability. In the Paradise of EIU the political friends and financial supporters are looked after first and the poor left to share the crumbs which might sustain a hand-to-mouth existence, but not life in any worthwhile sense of the word.

Making Sense of the Church and the World

The Old Testament model of a caring society is built around the concept of *shalom*. We associate that word with peace, but there is much more to it. It is the peace a community enjoys where there is justice, compassion and fairness. Two examples from Old Testament agricultural laws illustrate this point. Farmers were required to leave a margin in each field un-harvested. The grain or other crop remaining was there by right for the widow, the orphan and the alien! For the same reason fig trees could only be picked once in order to leave something for those in need. The essential point here is that there is a moral and human dimension to economic management, something often neglected in our current obsession with profit and efficiency.

Professor Elizabeth Cullen writing in the *Sunday Tribune* recently commented: 'Irish Society deteriorated during the reign of the Celtic Tiger not just because of the income shift but because people were more stressed and worked longer hours. There was an increase in depressive disorders and despite the doubling of incomes since 1989, no increase in life satisfaction.' We need as a society to rethink what constitutes a good standard of living and here the Churches can make a real contribution.

First of all by direct action. The Churches have a long tradition of active involvement in addressing the needs of people of all ages who for one reason or another find life difficult. These can be spiritual, emotional or material. There is a vast network of Church-sponsored support for those with special needs, including the homeless, refugees, substance abusers and many other vulnerable people. Such voluntary organisations can often take initiatives with groups on the margins of society who don't attract public sympathy or win votes for politicians and yet who have real needs... and rights.

Secondly by advocacy
Clergy and religious are among the remaining few 'professionals' who still live where they serve. They know the areas and they know the people. It is clear that people in authority dislike critical comment from churchmen and women, but it is difficult to dismiss the views of those who speak with knowledge and experience. It is vitally important that the churches sustain and encourage this prophetic role among its members, lay and ordained.

Experience suggests that a well-ordered and balanced society needs a level of public debate, which is independent of the organised political party system and other establishment interests. The churches, with the principles of human dignity and their experience, can play a major role in such a process and help sustain those signs of hope the world so desperately needs to see.

A POST-CATHOLIC IRELAND?

Ruairi Quinn

The words of Václav Havel seem remarkably applicable to the Irish today, 'Today, many things indicate that we are going through a transitional period when it seems that something is on the way out and something else is painfully being born. It is as if something were crumbling, decaying and exhausting itself, while something else, still indistinct, were arising from the rubble.' Ruairi Quinn's essay grapples with the changing face of Irish society today.

On Wednesday 29 August 1996 I was the host at a luncheon for a group of Irish-Americans in the windy city of Chicago. Francis Sheridan, the Irish Counsel General in that famous city had organised the event which took place in the executive club located on the top floor of the Amoco building, the second highest edifice in that quintessential mid-American city. As Minister for Finance, I was in town to promote the International Financial Services Centre on behalf of the IDA. As Deputy Leader of the Labour Party I was coincidentally there to attend the convention of the Democratic Party which nominated President Bill Clinton to run for a second term in the White House.

The combined agencies of the Irish state collaborated well together and in the full programme of my three day visit to

Chicago and Detroit, space and time was made available to meet with twenty or so Irish-Americans living in Chicago. At one stage, just before the great fire of the 1880s, Chicago, with forty per cent of its population coming from the island of Ireland, won out over Boston, Philadelphia and New York in their claims to be the pre-eminent Irish-American city. The political dominance of Mayor Richard Daly was a continuing testimony to that national legacy long after the primary position of the Irish-Americans had diminished as the majority of them moved up the social ladder and out of the city.

It was with representatives of this group that I now dined; successful, sophisticated, self-confident people. Some but not all had migrated to the United States in the dark days of the 1950s. Others were the children, even grandchildren, of earlier emigrants. Most had made visits back to Ireland. Everyone around that elegant table, superbly situated with spectacular views of Lake Michigan, was now aware of the incipient Celtic Tiger. They were content, at long last, to bask in the reflective success of the homeland that for so long was synonymous with poverty and failure. As we talked through the lunch, I responded to a series of questions about aspects of modern Ireland's economic and social performance. Then one clear steely edged question came from a person who had indicated earlier that they were an emigrant of the 1950s, a person who had left Ireland in my lifetime.

'Was not the country still dominated by the Catholic Church. Did the Bishops not still continue to exercise an overriding influence on society?' Whatever about economic success, he seemed to imply that we were still very much in awe of the Catholic hierarchy. I paused and reflected before my reply. Speaking in measured terms I looked at this man who was not much older than myself. Like me he would have had a memory, if not a direct experience, of the 'Mother & Child' controversy of the early 1950s. Here Church and State famously clashed and for many, but not all, Home Rule did seem like Rome Rule.

'You have to understand', I began, 'that economic change combined with increased international communications has had a big impact on social behaviour and attitudes. In that context I would say that today Ireland, that is the Republic of Ireland, is now a post-Catholic society'. Joe Carroll the *Irish Times* journalist present at the luncheon accurately reported my comments the following day, more by way of an aside than the central part of his article, which was about the relationship of the Irish government to either a Clinton White House or a Republican Bob Dole White House.

However, quite a number of people back in Ireland took considerable offence at my description of Ireland being post-Catholic, feeling that it was disrespectful of sincerely held belief within a significant section of the population. That was not what I was attempting to say even though Joe Carroll had reported my comments accurately. Fortunately, I was given an opportunity on an RTÉ programme entitled *What Really Matters* in February 1997 anchored by Olivia O'Leary to elaborate my view in the company of another Quinn. The other participant was David Quinn the ex-editor of *The Irish Catholic* and currently the religious correspondent of *The Irish Independent*. Ireland now, I offered the opinion, is a country of mixed belief and non-belief – so much so that no Irish government would feel compelled or obliged to consult exclusively with the Roman Catholic hierarchy in advance of introducing legislative proposals in a manner similar to what was the situation during the clash between the Bishops and the Cabinet over Noel Browne's proposals. David Quinn did not disagree. On the contrary, he broadly accepted my view yet remained uncomfortable, it seemed to me, with the consequences of my description.

Sr Stan belongs, as do I, clearly to a generation of Irish people who sang out resolutely and proudly the assertive lyrics of *A Nation Once Again* and *Faith of Our Fathers*. The Corpus Christi parade combined with the proliferation of white and yellow papal bunting was the seasonal signal that high summer was now upon us. The presence of a certainty everywhere, from Ballymena to Ballydehop, drove out intellectual or spiritual ambiguity and with that people who had real doubts. Clarity of mind and commitment to the cause, whatever it was, demanded complete and total allegiance.

On the top floor of the Amoco building, I got the sense that not all those who had left the shores of Ireland did so for economic reasons alone. Were ambivalent doubts about the certainty of their inherited beliefs also a contributing factor to their departure? Was the question posed to me as much a request for affirmation in their original decision to leave? Were they not right then and still not right now to have left that land of saints and scholars that had no space for them? If so, how could I possibly say that Ireland was now post-Catholic and by implication a safe place to which they could return?

The issue which they raised is for me an interesting one. We have, as a people, tended to generalise on the causes of emigration and the prevailing economic factors that drove so many people out from the newly independent state. We know now that there were other factors which were influential, but we do not have adequate statistics.

But let us start with the overt political emigration about which we do know. Unionists in the south, both Irish and British in nationality, did leave. Protestants, particularly in the

Ulster border counties such as Donegal, Cavan and Monaghan did so as well. At a British and Irish conference organised outside Washington DC in the late 1980s I met, for the first time, Jim Allister. He was a member of the DUP delegation and has now recently succeeded the Rev. Ian Paisley as the DUP member in the European Parliament. He told me, in Washington, that his people were originally from Monaghan but were driven across the border by their Catholic neighbours after 1922. The late Bob Cooper, a co-founder of the Alliance Party, was born in County Donegal but his family moved to the new Northern Irish state. Of course the traffic was in both directions. Many Catholics left or were burnt out of Belfast, for example, and came south. Such movements across new frontiers were common across the rest of Europe at that time. Margaret Macmillan's impressive history of the negotiations of the Parish Peace Conference 1919/1920, *The Peace Makers* contains many examples. These are, in most cases, self explanatory.

In the early 1930s, Peadar O'Donnell, the radical republican leader, had forced De Valera's hand on the disputed issue of land annuities and the 1921 Treacy requirement of their continued payment as part of the settlement. Dev clearly did not want to discontinue the payment when he came into office in 1932. Nevertheless he soon did and his action contributed to the commencement of the economic war between Britain and Ireland. During a heated debate later that decade about emigration and the social devastation which it was causing, Dev allegedly lashed back at O'Donnell. 'No matter who was in government', he asserted, 'a million people would have had to leave anyway'. 'Yes' responded Peadar, 'but with radical socialist policies in place, it would have been a different million'. As a young radical student activist I heard the story for the first time in the context of explaining the political and social conservatism that characterised the 1930s.

Was the Catholic Church in the new Free State the driving force of economic and social conservatism or did it merely reflect a predominantly rural conservative society? Can we even regard the Church at that time as a complete centrally controlled monolith. The two major religious components, the diocesan structure and the religious orders were on different, if even at that time, complementary paths.

The religious orders, both domestic and missionary, had a clarity of purpose and a place of commitment both socially and geographically that can still be seen to this day. It was the Catholic teaching orders who provided the secondary education infrastructure for the vast majority of the Catholic population of the new state. While many schools were in existence prior to 1922, their operations were consolidated significantly by the new independent state. The Christian Brothers, the Presentation nuns and the De la Salle Brothers along with the Dominicans and others catered, in the main, for that section of Irish society who could not afford to pay for the real or full cost of secondary education. Others, like the Sacred Heart and the Jesuits, along with, in my case the Holy Ghost Fathers, and the Vincentians played a more complex role. This was the education of the emerging Catholic middle class who were being groomed to take over control of the Protestant-dominated commanding heights of the Free State economy.

If we could beat them convincingly on the rugby pitch, then we could do so in business. In the mid 1920s the GAA tightened its rules in relation to the administration of the ban on foreign or garrison games. Blackrock College were informed, accordingly, that henceforth they could not have teams playing

Gaelic games as well as rugby in inter-school competitions. The priests, virtually all of whom have played Gaelic games in school and in the seminary, hardly hesitated in their choice. The confidence-building measures of repeated sporting success against such bastions of Protestant power as St Columbas, St Andrews, Wesley College and High School could not be abandoned.

What happened in education in the first few decades of independence was also happening in a similar way in our health and basic social services. Religious provision of hospitals and orphanages, along with correctional schools, were part of the Church's domestic mission. The religious orders provided the drive, expertise and personnel. The Bishops at government level and the parish priests at local level, delivered the political message to the politicians. Tight control was maintained and power clearly exercised.

But was that a victory for a driven church, or a capitulation by a supine lay society? Did one use the other, or were they happy to have it both ways? The delivery of educational health and social services came at a fraction of their full cost because of the management and labour contribution of the religious orders. Spiritual vocations had a real material value as far as the Department of Finance was concerned. Did it not suit the Cumann na nGael government in the twenties, and the Fianna Fàil government in the thirties to consolidate, in the early decades of independence, the clerically dominated infrastructure that imperial London had quietly acquiesced to after the 1801 Act of Union, and particularly after 1850?

Did the emotion and political energy of the nationalist movement deplete itself to the level of changing the colour of the post boxes, as some radical socialists asserted? Was the anti-clericalism of some members of Fianna Fáil, such as

Gerry Boland and Frank Aiken contained within the constraints of office and a driven desire to realise full political independence from Great Britain? John Horgan, in his biography of Sean Lemass, concludes that De Valera's successor was an agnostic. Yet he did not openly live that life and its values, unlike Todd Andrews who of course did not have to get elected.

Labour, to prove it was not communist had to be very Catholic. The Trade Union leaders, who dominated the parliamentary party right up until the end of the 1960s were in competition with Fianna Fáil. They were vulnerable on two fronts, nationalism and religion. Fianna Fáil, then as now, took no political prisoners. On the nationalist left, the republican congress of Peadar O'Donnell and George Gilmore were vanquished to the 1930s. Its natural successor, Clan na Phoblachta, had a similar faith nearly twenty years later.

Meanwhile, on the religious side, the Spanish civil war had an impact right across Europe and Ireland was no exception. The Catholic Church in Ireland unambiguously supported Franco's fascists. Anyone who disagreed with them was wrong, and anyone who fought with the international brigade was an enemy. Frank Edwards, an enthusiastic Waterford school teacher, lost his job in the Catholic national school when he returned from Spain having fought for democracy and against fascism. But the local Church extended the punishment to his mother by refusing her, very publicly, Holy Communion in Ballybricken's Catholic Church. Politics were intensely fought across Europe as we know. In addition the bitterness of the recent Irish civil war was still raw and any weapon, including a communist slur, was used to put down your opponent.

But no distinction was made between communism and socialism. Many in the Irish Catholic Church used the two words interchangeably in the same way that English people do with Britain and England. This ideological onslaught on the relatively weak Labour movement was happening before the Cold War and the threat of an atomic bomb attack. The Irish clergy, particularly those with links to continental Europe were well aware of the bitter ideological and political rivalry which was, even at that time, ongoing between socialist and communist parties in those continental countries. There was never a communist party of significance in Ireland but Labour had substantial support and clear democratic socialist credentials. The bitter ideological civil war within the left in Europe only concluded with the collapse of the Berlin Wall fifty years after Frank Edwards was sacked by the Church for fighting Franco and being a socialist.

Not just for unionists and protestants did the new Irish state become a cold place, to use David Trimble's phrase, but for socialists as well. By extension liberals and secularists could either put up or shove off. We know of the literary exiles who so publicly left such as Sean O'Casey, and those who so publicly never came back, such as James Joyce. What we do not know, and perhaps never can, is the number of spiritual exiles who ran away or were forced to leave. There can never be simple or single reasons for so many different and complex decisions, but I do believe that we can discern patterns.

In 1950, the ideology and the doctrine of the Catholic Church were used as a political battering ram to destroy Noel Browne's modest proposal contained in the Mother and Child Scheme. It's basic component deserves restatement – 'a universal service, free at the point of use, to all taxpayers and citizens for parents and their children up to the age of sixteen to be able to access their general practitioner and receive the appropriate primary care, including medicines'. As I write this in November 2004, Mary Harney, Tánaiste and recently appointed Minister for Health and Children, is defending her limited 'doctor only' visit card, confined to those in need. Fifty-four years later, the principle of universal service in medicine has no political validity with the government parties, Fianna Fàil and the Progressive Democrats. Furthermore, a country now rich beyond the wildest dreams of those members of that first Inter Party government is being told, without challenge, that the same level of universal service whose cost was not disputed in 1950, cannot be afforded in 2005.

There is no doubt that the conservatism of the medical profession in 1950 and the political adroitness of De Valera made clever use of that doctrinal battering ram and assisted its lethal propulsion. Likewise, the division of the Inter Party government and the personal rivalry between Browne and McBride were contributing factors.

While the rest of Europe slowly recovered from the ravages of World War II, Ireland languished. A booming Britain soaked up our spare labour. Of all the countries in Europe during the 1950s and 1960s, only two continued progressively to lose population, the Republic of Ireland and the German Democratic Republic. We know why the Germans were leaving and we believe that we know why the Irish had to go, but I suggest we do not have the full story. How many people fled Ireland in the wake of the fall out of the Mother and Child Scheme and their perception of clerical domination combined with political conservatism?

When I was Minister for Labour in 1983-1987, I established DÍON, the agency for support of Irish immigrants in Britain. Sadly there were high levels of emigration in those pre-Celtic Tiger days. As many as twenty-five thousand people were leaving the country, although up to seventeen thousand Irish immigrants were returning from Britain at the same time. The focus of attention and concern, however, was on those departing.

I met with a group of young Irish people in an Irish Centre in London who had taken the emigrant boat and I asked why they had left. Some were actually civil servants on a three-year career break from Ireland, anxious to see the world, escape from the narrowness of their native land and explore new options. Their security of return enabled them to travel. Others were unhappy, trapped and unable to live their lives as they saw it back in Ireland. The fact that they also found it very hard to get work in Ireland pushed them abroad. One young man, I recall, from Athlone was particularly bitter. Ireland was, in his words, 'a God forsaken place that had never done anything for him'. He was now unemployed in London, and blamed his jobless status on his lack of skills. When probed by me, he admitted that having been in the Irish Army Band in Athlone he had learned to play the trumpet. But he made no connection with that rare skill and its potential employment prospects within the Arts in London, which was then and is now the second largest economic sector after financial services in that cosmopolitan city. The third and final group were young educated professionals, who wanted to leave Ireland to get experience or simply felt that they had to get out from what they saw as a stifling, inward-looking and hypocritical country. Their experience of the aridity of the debate around the pro-life amendment of 1983 was frequently cited. The Ireland that they left was one in which they might be able to work, but not live.

Throughout Sr Stan's working life, the commitment to the marginalised in our society, from her or her many co-religious, has never been doubted. The option for the poor, an element of liberation theology, has frequently been articulated and lived out by dedicated individuals. The spiritual and religious vocations have found many causes and informed a passionate voice. Fr Sean Healy, the spokesperson for CORI, the Conference of Religious in Ireland, is the regular contributor on behalf of this group of religious orders. His constant denunciations were heard particularly of each of Charlie McCreevy's seven budgets. His criticisms of Fianna Fáil and Progressive Democratic policy which skewed income distribution within the best performing economy of Europe, if not the world, have become more strident with each year. But so impotent now is his voice and by extension that of the organisations he represents, that Fianna Fáil felt comfortable and secure in inviting him to address their pre-parliamentary retreat in Inchydoney in October 2004.

The defeat of a conscious pre-war secularism in the new modern state may have been the objective of the powers of the time within the Catholic Church such as Dr John Charles McQuaid, who uniquely bridged its two component parts. Archbishop of Dublin, the dominant diocese in the new state, he was also a former president of Blackrock College before his consecration. But in reference now to the current observance of Catholic practice and its social teaching the destruction of a conscious and openly secularist constituency within the young Republic of Ireland may very well be regarded, even from the point of view of the Catholic Church, as a pyrrhic victory.

Religious practice, if not belief, has dropped dramatically in recent years. Increased material wealth has, it is claimed by many, not brought about a happier or more spiritually content society. Young male suicide rates, binge drinking and marital breakdown are among the factors used as reference points to make this case. Indeed in posing this very question in the autumn of 2004, the Ombudsman, Emily O'Reilly, once regarded as a progressive journalist, suggested that perhaps we might be better off tip-toeing back into the churches from which we had fled. Breda O'Brien, an articulate Christian conservative journalist, applauded her former colleague's observation in a separate piece in the *Irish Times*. But neither of them attempted to suggest what they might hear in the Church that was any different or more convincing before it had been listened to self-evidently by so many officially and nominally of Catholic adherence.

Both of them had missed the point, as far as I am concerned. It is indifference and apathy which is killing the authority of the Church and not a conscious opposition to its message. The most Catholic of European countries has now the most unequal society, in terms of wealth distribution within the European Union. The triumph of individualism, tempered at best by a mean spirited means tested approach to social solidarity, is the ultimate victor to emerge.

Of course this reflects badly on the Labour movement and the broader socialist constituency in our society. As one of its leaders, I take my personal responsibilities seriously and recognise our own limitations in this struggle. But let it be understood that Ireland uniquely within Europe has never had a socialist led government, let alone a majority one. That we never got the chance to prove our full worth is a reflection upon us. Yet we were never even trusted, from the very beginning to be given that chance.

Mild, nice Jack Lynch, successfully toured the convents of Ireland in 1969, warning the then many and influential nuns of the dangers of Cuban communism! Brendan Corish, a devout Catholic, was fortunately not at home when his youngest son arrived home from school in tears, bullied because the teacher in St Peter's had described his father as a communist during that 1969 general election campaign. This was of course before we learned about the other activities which some male clerics of that historic diocese were visiting upon the young boys and girls in their charge.

As Ireland struggles, in the midst of its new found wealth to deal with the problems of success and excess, one clear positive legacy of Sr Stan's time shines through. The missionary tradition of solidarity with the Third World has, if anything, strengthened and reinforced itself while elsewhere clerical influence and Christian values as applied to society at home are in steep decline. Despite Bob Geldof's dismissive comments about Blackrock College, where he went to school, its missionary legacy, with him and others, is self-evident to this day. Bono's different Christian influences clearly inform his own consistent and energetic commitment to Third World debt relief and the achievement of the millennium goals. The large domestic cross party constituency for adherence to the UN target of 0.7 per cent by the year 2007, of Irish GDP, remains real-vocal and influential with the Irish electorate. The controversy over the Taoiseach's public and cavalier abandonment of a solemn promise made at the United Nations on behalf, not just of his government, but also in the name of the Irish people is a testimony to that Third World missionary legacy.

SAINT BRIGID'S PRAYER

Brendan Kennelly

As Brendan Kennelly's poem 'St Brigid's Prayer' reminds us there have been Irish women down through the ages who have made an invaluable contribution to the life of the Church and to the wider society.

(from the Irish)

I'd like to give a lake of beer to God.
I'd love the Heavenly
Host to be tippling there
for all eternity.

I'd love the men of Heaven to live with me,
to dance and sing.
If they wanted, I'd put at their disposal
vats of suffering.

White cups of love I'd give them
with a heart and a half;

sweet pitchers of mercy I'd offer
to every man.

I'd make Heaven a cheerful spot
because the happy heart is true.
I'd make the men contented for their own sake.
I'd like Jesus to love me too.

I'd like the people of Heaven to gather
from all the parishes around.
I'd give a special welcome to the women,
the three Marys of great renown.

I'd sit with the men, the women and God
there by the lake of beer.
We'd be drinking good health forever
and every drop would be a prayer.

WHY ARE THERE SO FEW WOMEN IN IRISH POLITICS?

Ursula Halligan

Inequality in Irish society presents itself in many forms. Ursula Halligan considers the seemingly perennial question of the under-representation of women in Irish politics.

As questions go, it's a hardy annual. Every year someone somewhere asks why there are so few women in Irish politics and every year the political parties respond with the same old hand-wringing and head-scratching. Yes, they say it's regrettable that while 51 per cent of the population is made up of women only 13 per cent of TDs are women. Yes, it's unfortunate that the number of women in the Dail has risen by just one percent in the last ten years and yes they admit, at this rate of going it will take 370 years before the number of women in the Dail reaches the 50 per cent mark.

On paper at least, political parties support equality for women in politics. Over the years Ireland has signed many European treaties and international covenants committing the government to equal opportunities for women in political and public decision-making. Like motherhood and apple pie, it's a hard one to oppose. On grounds of fairness, equity and balance, it makes sense that women, who constitute half the population and possess different life experiences to men, should have an equal input into decision-making at the highest level.

Only problem is, it's not happening. Women predominate in local, voluntary and community groups, but virtually disappear off the radar when it comes to the national political scene. Today, out of 166 TDs, only twenty-two are women. Ten counties still have no female TD and Ireland rates a poor fifty-ninth out of 120 nations in terms of parliamentary representation of women.

Political parties say they actively recruit female candidates but that women are slow to come forward. Last June, the dearth of female candidates in Fianna Fáil was clear for all to see when the party ran an all-male slate of candidates in the European Elections.

Off the record, some male TDs will quietly tell you that women are their own worst enemies. They're not pushy enough, they say, and men are naturally more aggressive. Women lack the necessary drive, ambition and confidence to succeed and they add, many aren't that interested in politics anyway.

It's a view that's not a million miles away from the old, misogynistic belief that women are biologically ill-disposed to a career in politics or business. Such a belief can be traced back to the eighteenth century when scientists concluded that because males' skulls were larger than females' skulls and females' pelvises were larger than males' pelvises, men were better suited for politics, business, and public life, and women, whose smaller skulls were interpreted as indicating lesser intelligence, were best suited to bearing children and looking after the home.

Two centuries later, the same scientists might be amazed to learn that women's little brains have turned in a better performance that they'd have predicted. Right across the board, girls are doing better than boys at school. Here in Ireland they outperform boys in virtually every Leaving Cert. subject at honours level, including subjects like maths and science, traditionally considered bastions of male superiority. Women are also ahead of men in the third level education league. In 2002, six out of ten graduates were women.

You might think such academic achievement would automatically ensure success or at least equal representation in the political and business spheres but you'd be wrong. The abysmal under-representation of women in the Dáil is not confined to politics. It's the same old story in business, banking, medicine, law, all the professions, industry and the media. Nowhere are women key decision-makers.

Only 3 per cent of chief executives are female. Irish women may have better Leaving Certs than their male colleagues, but they're earning less and not rising to the top of their chosen professions. The latest CSO figures (December 2004) show that women earn, on average, two-thirds what men earn. The number of men earning more than €50,000 a year was over 115,000 while just 25,000 women exceeded that amount. More women are also poorer than men. In fact, the proportion of women at risk of poverty in 2001, after pensions and social transfers, was 23 per cent, the highest in the EU. Roughly, 80 per cent of workers in the lowest paid jobs – catering, caring and cleaning – are women.

It's all very confusing. Women are beating the pants off boys in the classroom, but as soon as they go out into the big bad world, everything goes pear-shaped for them. It's something that baffles political parties too. So much so that Fianna Fail commissioned a Gender, Equality Audit to find out what's really going on.

In January 2005, the audit published its report with an action plan and a foreword written by the Taoiseach. In it, Bertie

Ahern acknowledged that Irish politics was indeed largely 'a man's world' and that the very significant under-representation of women in society 'impoverishes our democracy.' He said it must change and that Fianna Fáil must lead the way. 'In theory, the Irish political playing pitch may be level but in practice, it is a lot more difficult for women to get on to it,' he wrote.

The audit report published the result of an attitude survey in which two thousand party members were presented with a list of potential obstacles to women participating in politics. Respondents were asked to rate the factors from 'very significant' to 'insignificant'.

The obstacle that drew the highest 'very significant' response (63.8%) was the one that said: 'men have better support networks/connections in Fianna Fail'.

The obstacle that drew the next highest response was the vaguely titled 'other' category (53.8%). The report noted that most comments in this category made by women respondents referred to a combination of structures and attitudes in Fianna Fail working against women. It quotes the following examples verbatim: 'men in FF find it hard to accept women'; 'the closed shop attitude of existing representatives'; 'no real commitment to getting women involved'; 'older members of FF think women should be at home'.

Lack of affordable child-care facilities was the third biggest obstacle listed (50.2%). As a result of the report, Fianna Fail set itself a ten-year target to ensure that women comprise one in every three candidates for local and general elections.

At one level, this is laudable and interesting. It's even encouraging that Fianna Fail commissioned such an audit (even if the money (€105,000) that paid for it was a financial incentive under the National Development Plan). At another level, though, it has to be asked if such a report was ever necessary.

After all, isn't it blindingly obvious why so few women are in politics? Isn't it patently evident why women are under-performing everywhere except in the classroom? – It's hardly rocket science. In fact, 'it's biology, stupid' and if there was a scientific equation to sum it all up, it might go like this: someone has to have society's babies. Women are the ones with the wombs. Babies are hard work; take up lots of time and are expensive to rear. Shared parenting is a myth and childcare facilities cost a fortune. Society and government do little or nothing to support motherhood. Ergo, if you're a woman who gets married and has children, chances are you can forget about a high-powered career or putting your brilliant Leaving Cert. to use. QED.

Men generally don't face any of these difficulties. On the whole, marriage tends to work very nicely for them – and their careers. Marriage allows men the freedom to pursue advantage in their working lives and dominate the powerful, decision-making positions in society because someone else is holding the baby. It's little wonder that respondents to the Fianna Fail survey cited the support systems available to male TDs as the biggest obstacle to women's political advancement.

It's not uncommon to hear male TDs with several children expressing regret about how much time they miss with their family before quickly praising their wives and partners for the way they free the male TDs to do their job. Female TDs rarely have quite so committed a support system back home. It's hardly insignificant that two of the three female Cabinet Ministers, and the only female Minister of State are all childless – or child-free, if you want a more neutral term.

The lack of a support system for working mothers is a recurring theme in comments made by female TDs when they are asked why there are so few women into politics.

Fine Gael's Olivia Mitchell TD (Dublin South) doesn't put a tooth in it: 'It's biology, biology, biology. Our biology is against us. You're bearing and rearing a family during the years when you should be building a career – in any career – but particularly politics where it's so one hundred per cent and the hours are appalling. If women want to go into politics they have to be desperately lucky like I was that the opening was there when I had my kids virtually reared'.[1]

In the last general election Marie Hoctor (Tipperary North) was the only new woman in Fianna Fáil elected to the Dáil. Upon entering Leinster House, Hoctor says she suddenly realised she was unique politically for another reason too. 'It was Mary Coughlan who pointed out to me that I had broken the mould because (currently) I'm the only woman elected to FF in the Dáil who didn't either have a husband, uncle or some other male relative in the Oireachtas before me.'

Hoctor says the fact that she is not married and doesn't have children makes political life easier for her, although not as easy as men have it. She remembers one incident when she was a councillor in Tipperary and the Fianna Fáil group asked her at extremely short notice to do a quick report. Later that evening she received a call from a fellow male Fianna Fáil councillor demanding to know where the report was. 'I said I hadn't done it yet. He said 'why not?' in an accusing tone. I said, ' because I'm cooking my own dinner, something you didn't have to do''.

Hoctor says it's also hard for women to get into politics because they're up against so many long-established male dynasties. 'Politics has been a male reserve for so long. It's so hard to break what has been the tradition. Don't underestimate the fact that those who go before us (ie those already elected) have quite a say in those who will succeed them... and men (generally) perpetuate men'.[2]

Former Fine Gael TD Madeleine Taylor Quinn was the first woman to be elected to an officership in the Fine Gael Party in 1979. While in the Senate in 1994, she gave her colleagues a taste of what political life is like for a working mother. 'If a woman politician who delivers a child takes fourteen weeks' leave the reality is that the males in her constituency will have taken every opportunity to do a hatchet job on her. I am sure the Minister will have to use all his brain power and that of his officials to try to get around that difficulty because I do not see how women politicians can be treated equally given the nature of the political game. I am speaking from experience as I gave birth to two children while a member of Dáil Eireann and I know exactly what I am talking about. The maximum I could afford to spend out of circulation was two weeks'.[3] Speaking to women involved in public life in central and Eastern Europe, the former Minister of State and current Progressive Democrat TD, Liz O'Donnell described Irish politics as 'neither woman nor family-friendly' and 'tailor-made for men with supportive wives'.[4]

All of these comments make it sound like women with career or political ambitions could do with a wife. The reality for most women is that while more of them are working outside the home than ever before (60%), they are still the primary childcarers as well as the ones who do all the washing-up, mopping up, hovering, cooking, shopping and picking up the children from school, sports practice, music lessons and other extra-curriculum activities. Many women work shorter hours in paid employment than men only because they've got a second unpaid (and often more demanding) job to go to at home.

In recent years an army of immigrant nannies, babysitters and cleaners help them keep the show on the road, but it's often a costly, unsatisfactory and stressful way of living. It frequently means that working-women get the worst of both worlds. Hassled at home, harried at work, they end up missing out on either a wholesome family life or a satisfying career.

At this point, male cynics might exclaim: 'What a bunch of complaining idiots. Why don't women make up their minds and decide what they really want? Stay at home or get a paid job?' The truth is most women don't have a choice. Quite apart from the high cost of living and the need for a second income in most homes, it's also Government and EU policy (the so-called Lisbon agenda) to get more women into the workplace. The Government needs extra women working because the country has a labour shortage. A shortage of labour raises costs (salaries), which renders the economy less competitive. That's why the Government has set itself a target to increase the number of women working in paid employment to 70 per cent. A few years ago Charlie McCreevy changed the tax system (i.e. individualisation) in a way that effectively penalises couples where only one person works outside the home.

For years feminists have resisted the notion that biology is destiny. That's why contraception and even abortion became feminist issues. Many women want to control their fertility so that they're not reduced to baby machines dependent on the goodwill of men. The reality is that until the day comes when either: a) a new bio-technology frees women from the social disadvantages of their biology: or b) men suddenly do a somersault and agree to take on a fairer share of childcare and domestic duties, women who get married and have children will be forever stuck in a dependent head-lock with their male partners.

The usual panacea demanded by women's groups, namely more childcare places, may not be the ideal solution. Recent studies suggest that very young children, between the ages of one and three, need a strong loving presence in their lives during these early years if they are to develop into healthy, well-adjusted adults, but a strong loving presence doesn't have to be the mother. Fathers qualify for that role too.

Equal parenting or shared parenthood may be a myth right now, but it would be the perfect solution to the battle of the sexes if men and women could negotiate a fairer trade when they agree to hitch up together instead of the lopsided system that currently exists and which so manifestly favours the male/husband.

It is only when such a seismic shift occurs in the relations between husbands and wives, men and women that we may hope to see more women in politics and positions of power. Former President, Mary Robinson put down her own marker for recognising when that day has come: 'I look forward to the day when women's participation in all levels of government will be an unremarkable feature of public life. We will know that there is true equality when the last obstacles are overcome, when women are as free to make mistakes as men and not have it blamed on their gender!'[5]

Notes

1. Interview with author 7 January, 2005.
2. Interview with author 7 January, 2005.
3. Seanad Eireann Official Report, vol.141 Privilege and Immunity Bill, 1994. Col 1255. Quoted in *Women in Parliament. Ireland: 1918-2000* by Maedhbh McNamara and Pascal Mooney.
4. *Irish Times*, 23 June 2000.
5. Mary Robinson, former president of Ireland quoted from the preface in *Women in Parliament*. 2000 Op cit.)

SOLID PUDDING AGAINST EMPTY PRAISE: GLIMPSES OF JUSTICE, PLAYFULNESS AND ROLE REVERSAL

Lelia Doolan

Amidst the many problems which beset Irish society today it is important not to forget that there are many positives: people and acts of kindness, goodness and compassion that fan the flames of all that is good in Irish life and helps all of us grow into the fullness of our humanity. Lelia Doolan sees 'Glimpses of Justice, Playfulness and Role Reversal'.

> Poetic justice, with her lifted scale,
> Where, in nice balance, truth with gold she weighs,
> And solid pudding against empty praise.
> > *The Dunciad* Pope.

How many officers of the law have broken those laws or spent time in jail as part of their training? I exclude such unique judicial types as Rumpole of the Bailey and Judge John Deed.

Bertolt Brecht rejoiced in turning the social system upside down to dramatise and satirise the hypocrisies of public morals. The judge in *The Caucasian Chalk Circle*, for instance, has been a notorious robber. He now dispenses justice with an even hand. In one scene, he must exert the wisdom of Solomon between a rich and a poor woman in the matter of motherhood of a child. Years ago I saw a great production of the play, by the Strand Players, in Mountjoy jail. I've seldom been among an audience who so obviously savoured the justice of the outcome when Grusha's mothering compassion, and not the privileged legal possessiveness of the Marquise, was publicly acknowledged.

Would those Mountjoy prisoners emerge from their victimhood with that judge's engaged detachment? Or would their resentment consign them simply to the cul-de-sac of individual self-interest in a society apparently more and more devoted to the protection of its own privileged groups?

Do trainee doctors spend hours in waiting rooms? Do bankers have their loans denied; are bishops refused forgiveness? How many civil servants and politicians take a regular sabbatical among the homeless, immigrants, the disabled, the elderly poor or the drug-addicted among us?

Not many. What practical value is there in any of that, they might say. Pinko fantasising...

Once upon a time, in the not-so-long ago, social arrangements were interestingly varied. There were egalitarian societies such as hunter-gatherer/pastoralist bands, rank societies and chiefdoms where inequality in social standing and access to economic resources were kept to a minimum. And although some persons might be better hunters or more skilled artists there was still equal access to status positions for persons of the same ability. These groups also depended on sharing, ensuring equal access to economic resources in spite of any acquired prestige. In a chiefdom, although the rank is likely to be hereditary, high status is marked by giving wealth away rather than by keeping it. Such redistribution, usually of food or goods, signifies that the wealth is communally held. Many a chief emphasises his position through the raggedness and impoverishment of his appearance.

And there were and are societies, such as our own stratified society of today, where access to social status and to economic resources is socially structured to be unequal and dependent on class or caste.

Ways of maintaining a just order in these societies obviously differ as well. It might be achieved through action on the part of the whole community / society or through the use of informal adjudicators – even though these may not have the power to enforce their decisions. Another way is through oaths and ordeals (And woe betide the witch in those days, the dissident in these.) In societies such as our own, disputes are usually resolved and misdemeanours punished through the use of codified laws and courts, particularly for those with unequal access to both social standing and economic resources.

The 'simple' systems for ensuring fair play in egalitarian societies might appear to be largely irrelevant to our twenty-first century complexity. They seem hardly to offer a clue to solving the mystery of a fair social order. Yet, hidden within our immense mega-polity are social inventions which stretch, again and again, longingly towards those models: formal and informal groupings of fire-fighters, operating egalitarian systems of rescue for those excluded from the phantom of 'progress'; systems which then become, in time, part of the social structure itself.

People whose subversive imagination can cause uproar, whose acuteness and passion drives them toward alerting us to these imbalances, who create new possibilities are artists of the spirit, surprising and imaginative. Equally, they can be playful and angry. A cousin of mine had her work in helping disabled young people get an education in a small African village terminated, while she was temporarily away, by a local priest (on grounds of 'rationalisation'). She wrote that she hoped her anger would endure until she had had a chance to discuss matters with the bishop. Such righteous anger is too often dismissed as excessive. It is, to my mind, the vital engine that redresses. Maybe, as has been suggested, modern therapy has converted anger into anxiety.

In modern societies there are few formally structured public opportunities for deriding injustice and puncturing self-importance. The custom of publicising an implied injustice by fasting on the doorstep of the noble detractor probably had one of its last major performances during the farmers' march in Dublin in 1966. Anomalies and perceived injustices are nowadays packaged for the media who undertake a function as public mediators under the glare of a hastily ticking clock.

A formal, socially controlled example of role/power reversal occurs among the Lohti people in Zambia. There, the drummers in the Barotse royal barge were entitled annually to throw into the water any of the noble entourage who had offended them and their sense of justice during the year. It signified the power of the weak. I'm sure it also gave the drummers a good laugh. In universities, in the past, the annual rag had remnants of the same spirit when lecturers might be kidnapped and sequestered, or other excesses might break out. A lot of that energy seems to have evaporated recently or been subsumed into the safety (however inventive) of street theatre.

Protest marches, such as those against the Irish government's involvement in the invasion of Iraq, are an example of social solidarity across classes and ages. Their participants' inability to wield sufficient social or economic power, however, and thus to alter the government's action, confined their gesture to the symbolic (memorable and important as this was and is). Just as enabling the porters, secretaries, restaurant and bar staff within the Oireachtas building ritually to bar the doors to deputies and organise an alternative parliament (with legislative powers!) on an annual basis might add an astringent element to our democracy.

Other characteristics, like the Irish propensity for ignoring social responsibility when it come to money and property (mine), for granting the absolution of amnesia to violent acts committed in the name of 'freedom', for diddling local and central government (not yet internalised by many citizens as having anything to do with me and you and our responsibilities to one another) are balanced by considerable charitable magnanimity towards all forms of disaster, wherever they occur. It is as if, in these instances, we wish to admit to no social authority other than that of our own generous impetuosity.

Within these arresting contradictions and imbalances (truth against gold; solid pudding against empty praise) stands the work and the person honoured in these pages. She has galvanised Irish society for over half a century by laughing at howling chasms of inequality, making mischief with injustice and creating new social groupings and hopes through the steady, patient/impatient whirl of her mystical wings.

Given that example, we could do worse than take flight, too. As William Stafford says:

> There are people in every country who never
> turn into killers, saints have built
> sanctuaries on islands and in valleys
> conquerors have quit and gone home, for thousands
> of years farmers have worked the fields.
> My feet begin the uphill curve
> Where a thicket spills with birds every spring.
> The air doesn't stir. Rain touches my face.

We could do worse than take heart, too.

FAITH AND RENEWAL IN THE VALLEY OF THE RHINE

Sarah McDonald

*The Church has found innumerable forms to show people the sacred –
in painting, music, sculpture, stained glass and architecture. Yet how
many times are female images other than Mary used? The exclusion of
the feminine experience often appears an unanswerable conundrum
for those who believe in gender equality and it often rouses us to anger.
Sarah McDonald's article reminds us that women such as Hildegard
of Bingen have consistently surfaced in the history of the Christian
Church to play an important role in social, economic and political
affairs.*

The biggest event in the Church's 2005 calendar – World Youth
Day – is to be held in Cologne. World Youth Day gatherings are
occasions of joy, goodwill and celebration. The spectacle
affords jaded believers an opportunity to witness the
enthusiasm and religious fervour which Catholicism continues
to inspire among young people around the world. The occasion
may also counter some of the scepticism about the relevance of
the Church's message to young people.

At World Youth Day in Rome in 2000, Pope John Paul,
quoting from the fourteenth-century saint, Catherine of Siena,
told the two million young people gathered before him: 'If you

are what you should be, you will set the whole world ablaze.'

If the Pope is looking for a reflection to inspire the young people who attend the Papal Mass in Cologne, he may be moved to draw from some of the significant religious figures associated with the city. When I think of Cologne, I think specifically of three monumental female figures in Church history. All women embodying Christian solidarity with deeply prayerful lives, all underlining the fact that from the earliest stages of the Church's history, independent women have always played their part.

Cologne is of course the setting for one of the most inspiring stories of Christian martyrdom. It was here, according to legend, that St Ursula and her 11,000 companions were slaughtered at the hands of the Huns in the fourth century.

While St Ursula's legend may at this stage seem rather remote and rather too fantastical to be credible, it does underline that religious women were not expected to be shrinking violets if anything, the more courageous and independent they were, the more they inspired others, even at the highest echelons of the Church. Think of the impact she is reputed to have had on Pope Cyriacus, who chose to abdicate the papacy and die a martyr amongst her entourage.

Of course her influence did not end with her death. Centuries later she was still inspiring men and women, notably St Angela Merici, the sixteenth-century foundress of the Ursuline congregation and pioneer of the first unenclosed female religious order and advocate of women's education and religious formation.

An altogether more contemporary female figure for whom Cologne was of central importance and whose prescient views on women's contribution to society and the Church are proving increasingly relevant today, was the Jewish philosopher,

Christian feminist and Carmelite mystic, St Edith Stein. She was selected by Pope John Paul as one of three co-patronesses of the Church in October 1999.

Her faith journey brought her from Judaism to agnosticism to Catholicism. She was baptised in Cologne's Cathedral Church on I January 1922. Her decision to join the Discalced Carmelite monastery in Cologne in 1933, was in part the culmination of a journey of searching but it was also spurred by the fact that her lecturing position was no longer open to her on account of the Nazi race laws which robbed many Jews and Jewish converts of their professions.

In the wake of Kristallnacht, she left the Carmelites in Cologne to go to another monastery in Holland, in the hope that her Cologne community would be safer in her absence. However, as the Nazi regime tightened its stranglehold on Europe, her safety in Holland became less secure. In the wake of the Dutch bishops' letter protesting against the treatment of the Jews, the Nazis responded brutally and swiftly, rounding up all Catholics in Holland of Jewish descent, including Edith and her sister Rosa Stein. She was murdered in Auschwitz in August 1942.

In 1999 Pope John Paul declared that the proclamation of Edith Stein as a co-patroness of Europe 'is intended to raise on this continent a banner of respect, tolerance and acceptance which invites all men and women to understand and appreciate each other, transcending their ethnic, cultural and religious differences in order to form a truly fraternal society.'

Recognising humanity's interdependence was a central theme of yet another extraordinary mystic who hailed from Cologne's hinterland. The twelfth-century German Benedictine abbess, Hildegard of Bingen, often referred to as the Sibyl of the Rhine, is only now beginning to be acknowledged as one of the truly creative minds of the medieval Church. The versatility of Hildegard's intellectual interests is underlined by the wide spectrum of disciplines with which she concerned herself. This is best underlined by the large corpus of her written material which has survived, including her three mystical treatises: *Know the Ways*, *The Book of Divine Works* and *The Book of Life's Merits*. She also compiled *Causes and Cures*, a medical compendium of her observations concerning the biology of the human body, its illnesses and their cure. Another scientific work, *Natural History*, documents the trees, plants and rocks she utilised in her role as a healer. Her creative work includes poetry and music. Considered to be one of, if not the first female composer in Western music, Hildegard composed seventy-seven liturgical songs and a musical drama, *Ordo Virtutem*.

For Hildegard, musical composition had a sacred function. 'Musical harmony softens hard hearts inducing in them the moisture of contrition and summons the Holy Spirit.' Despite little or no musical training, her reputation as a composer had already spread by 1148, as attested by a letter commending her originality from the Parisian magister, Ordo of Soissons.

Who was Hildegard of Bingen? She was born in Bermersheim, Germany in 1098, to a noble family, the tenth of ten children. From an early age, mystical experiences formed an integral part of her life, and it may have been on account of these divine insights that her parents sent her at the very young age of eight, to the care of an anchoress at the Benedictine monastery in Disibodenberg. The monastery had been re-founded in 1105 in the wake of the monastic reform movement emanating from the Benedictine abbey at Cluny in Burgundy. With her spiritual formation assigned to Jutta of Spanheim, Hildegard was given an education which most of her contemporaries wouldn't have had access to. Academically, however, it would not have been to the same rigorous standards as those reserved for the monks of the monastery.

When she was fifteen, Hildegard became a Benedictine nun and following the death of Jutta in 1136, she was elected by the other members of the community as superior. Jutta alone had been privy to the knowledge of Hildegard's mystical experiences and their accompanying illnesses, which left her charge debilitated. However, she had informed Volmar, the nuns' spiritual director, of their existence and it was to Volmar that Hildegard turned when in 1141, she received the divine command to record her visions. As Hildegard wrote: 'In the forty-third year of my life's course, when in a heavenly vision in great fear, I saw the greatest radiance in which was formed a voice from Heaven saying to me: Oh frail human, ash of ash and corruption of corruption – tell and write what you see and hear.'

Volmar recognised the divine inspiration behind her visions and set about assisting Hildegard in the transcription of what was to become the first of three major works of mystical treatises. In all, *Scivias* or *Know the Ways* took ten years, from 1141 to 1151, to complete. In the meantime, Hildegard wrote to St Bernard of Clairvaux, one of the leading proponents of the second crusade and an advocate of the monastic reform movement, to seek his advice as to whether she should publicly disclose the details of her visions. This letter, dating from 1147 is the earliest extant letter of hers. St Bernard's favourable response was to mark the beginning of Hildegard's public life.

As word spread about her mystical visions and prophetic powers she was sought out for her advice on a range of issues. However, sometimes her advice was not so much sought as sent. Amongst her letters of correction and advice, which survive are letters to Pope Anastasius IV, Emperor Frederick Barbarossa and King Henry II of England, as well as to bishops, nuns and members of the laity.

The twelfth century was an unsettled and changing one, where schism, antipopes and crusades were symptomatic of the tension existing between the ecclesiastical and temporal powers. Hildegard's assertion that 'Peace has to be sought for with difficulty in a changeable world and can be preserved only with difficulty', was particularly pertinent to this period of history, and holds true for the twenty-first century just as readily. In all, some of Hildegard's letters survive, and they serve to highlight the way she attempted through these missives to apply the cosmology of her revelations in a practical manner.

Fundamental to Hildegard's mysticism was the emphasis she laid on the complementarity of the elements of creation. Rather than viewing humanity and nature, mankind and the cosmos, body and soul, as disparate entities – she sought to underline their interconnectedness.

In Hildegard's cosmos, God is the source of everything, and for this reason, she did not fear science, but emphasised the good to which it could be put. Perhaps this is why she took such an interest in medicine and physiology.

What is most surprising to the modern reader of Hildegard's works is the relevance of her message, despite its antiquity, to the concerns of the twenty-first century. Most unusual is her insight into what we now term creation spirituality – best summed up in her use of the concept of *viriditas* or greenness, which is representative of the creative power present in nature and having its source in God. Humanity, according to Hildegard, despite its special place in creation, has a special responsibility to nature, and abuse of its position could upset this dynamic of interdependence. In her estimation, humanity was entrusted with a caretaker role. 'God created mankind so that mankind might cultivate the earthly and thereby create the heavenly.' Amen.

ENVOI

Eavan Boland

Appropriately Eavan Boland's poem 'Envoi' combines themes of Easter, renewal, feminity and creativity.

It is Easter in the suburb. Clematis
shrubs the eaves and trellises with pastel.
The evenings lengthen and before the rain
the Dublin mountains become visible.

My muse must be better than those of men
who made theirs in the image of their myth.
The work is half-finished and I have nothing
but the crudest measures to complete it with.

Under the street-lamps the dustbins brighten.
The winter flowering jasmine casts a shadow
outside my window in my neighbour's garden.
These are the things that my muse must know.

She must come to me. Let her come
to be among the donnée, the given.
I need her to remain with me until
the day is over and the song is proven.

What I have done I have done alone.
What I have seen is unverified.
I have the truth and I need the faith.
It is time I put my hand in her side.

If she will not bless the ordinary,
if she will not sanctify the common,
then here I am and here I stay and then am I
the most miserable of women.

LOVE STRIKES

Kathy Sinnott

Kathy Sinnott MEP is, like Sr Stan and Peter McVerry, one of Ireland's best known campaigners for those on the margins of society, for those who are sometimes treated, in her own words as 'enemies of the state'. She showcases a hidden talent for short story writing in the gently humorous 'Love Strikes'.

Mrs Higgins smiled just as John did when he heard his father opening the door after work. What would come next? A hair tousling, a hug or 'So Chief, any fires today?'

Best of all was being scooped up against his cold coat and carried into the kitchen and crushed between his parents when they kissed. He would squirm, but it was heaven.

But Mrs Higgins was not an excited child like him. She was old. It was hard to place Mrs Higgins. She was a bit family, but only a bit because everyone, even his Nana, called her Mrs Higgins. She was part of birthdays and Christmas and everyday. She had the room at the end of the hall, but he never went into it even in the night when he was cold because of her being only a bit family.

'A very curious boy,' his Nana said. He knew the contents of all the cupboards, but he didn't know what Mrs Higgins' room looked like or what was in it except that there was St Joseph. She carried St Joseph into the living room in March for his novena.

It was at the novena that she smiled at St Joseph like he smiled at his father. Each day of the nine days that constituted the novena, she smiled more until her face was like his when his father was walking in or it was his birthday or when he had been good and mother had promised to tell father.

He didn't think about Mrs Higgins' smile but just saw it and put it away to think about later. He was busy being a fireman. He forgot to think about it until he himself was walking in the door to little ones beaming and breathless and wriggling like puppies.

He thought about Mrs Higgins and about St Joseph, the 'Foster Father'. He missed his own father now that he had children. He was ready to be fostered. Had she been fostered?

Clare was young when she was sent from Newry though she was 'older' than her three brothers and wee sister. Her father's death had put an abrupt end to her brief childhood. A brother was older, but couldn't be spared to come with her. He had to stay home to be the man of the house.

She arrived by boat to America and by train to Chicago, dressed in her Sunday clothes and carrying a statue of St Joseph in her work dress. She was strong for her age and was hired immediately. She worked hard and spent nothing, sending every dollar home. Her mother wrote frequently giving her the news and always thanking God and His Holy Mother and Clare for the money she sent.

Her mother's letters were long and detailed. Clare was part of every joy and disappointment, every milestone and set-back. She lived her family life through these letters written and read with St Joseph in her little space. Clare relied on him for everything, whispered to him and he listened. Her sister recovered from croup and the others were spared.

Her middle brother got the writing prize and one by one they found jobs and married. Grandchildren began to arrive and her advice was sought on names. Clare always put the question to St Joseph. Every family eventually had a Joseph or Josie. There was worry, excitement and achievement. Then there was death. After her mother's death there was silence.

Clare was forty-two. Like herself, her dollars were orphaned. For the first time they began to fill the little handkerchief box on her dresser. She asked for news, she begged for letters. She was more surprised at St Joseph's silence than her family's. They were busy with their children and jobs, but he, what did he have to do? He had never been too busy to listen before. He had never ignored her requests for help like this.

One morning she woke with a new prayer which she asked with all the confidence of a best friend. 'Father Joseph, a husband'. Every night the husband became more real. St Joseph was put in no doubt. He was to be Irish, kind, non-drinking, hard-working, funny, respectable-looking, fortyish and Catholic.

She watched and waited. She was conscious of every stranger at dawn Mass, at her employer's door and at the store. Which one of the men she passed would it be? She was eager to know – but happy to be patient.

Over the next three years, she became more flexible. She dropped the 'funny' first and then the 'respectable-looking'. There are many good men in dirty work clothes and why should she restrict St Joseph's search to a certain age group? It was hard to release the 'non-drinker', she heard so many stories. The last to go were the Irish and the kind. For another year she begged and bargained for her Catholic man.

She was forty-six and getting impatient. For the first time in her life, she began to wheedle and nag, 'Why do you give me everything I ask for but the one thing I want?'

It had been a particularly close, trying day and she had had to be pleasant and submissive for her 'Tuesday and Thursday family' who were themselves having a trying day. It was late and hot. Clare was hungry, lonely and every flight of stairs sharpened the edge. Even before she lightened the room she was aware of St Joseph turned to the wall. She had not been talking to him for a few days but it had done no good and he didn't seem to mind. She turned him around and unleashed her frustration. When she could think of nothing more she hissed 'Mother said you would take care of me.' Exhausted she screamed, 'Where is my husband?' and sent St Joseph flying through her window.

She was shaking when she heard the scream and thump on the street below. Running to the window and leaning out she saw a man lying across the sidewalk.

She married Mr Higgins before Christmas. He was a kind, non-drinking, hard-working, forty-four year old Irish Catholic who had a quiet sense of humour, a respectable look and a deep devotion to St Joseph.

THE GIFT

Brendan Kennelly

Kathy Sinnott's theme of unexpected and wonderful surprises finds a suitable echo in Brendan Kenelly's poem, 'The Gift'.

It came slowly.
Afraid of insufficient self-content
Or some inherent weakness in itself
Small and hesitant
Like children at the tops of stairs
It came through shops, rooms, temples,
Streets, places that were badly-lit.
It was a gift that took me unawares
And I accepted it.

ANALYSING A FEMINIST ETHIC OF CARE: A POTENTIAL IRISH MODEL?

Helena O'Riordan Keleher

As Denis Hickie reminds us in his preface to this book one of Sr Stan's many valuable contributions to Irish society has been to encourage the development of young people through her work in the Young Social Innovators. Accordingly, it was important to bring a young and fresh voice to this collection. Helena O'Riordan Keleher is a recent theology graduate and in her essay considers the importance of an 'ethic of care'.

In 1982, an American sociologist Carol Gilligan published *In A Different Voice: Psychological Theory and Women's Development*.[1] It was a book that had such an effect on feminism that its ripples are still being felt today. It sold over 750,000 copies and has been translated into seventeen different languages. I wish to discuss some of the arguments put forth by Carol Gilligan because I feel very strongly that these issues will continue to challenge the field of social work and formulation of public policy in the future. Gilligan's work has become the 'classic statement of feminist ethics'.

In 1970 Carol Gilligan was a student of Lawrence Kohlberg at Harvard University. Kohlberg was well known for his 'stage theory' in developmental psychology, and one thing Gilligan noticed while working with him was that women consistently scored lower on his moral development tests than men.[2] Did this mean that women were less morally developed? It turned out that Kohlberg's subjects were primarily privileged white men and boys, and Gilligan posited that this was skewing Kohlberg's results. If you come up with a theory of moral development using only a small subset of society, then that theory can't be applied to everyone. Maybe women weren't less morally developed, maybe their morality simply developed differently?

Gilligan's model of feminine ethics came to be called an 'ethic of care'. It was based, broadly, around research she conducted. It showed that boys seemed to make moral decisions based on absolute principles of right and wrong, and identified themselves by distinguishing themselves from others by their achievements. In contrast, Gilligan suggested that girls tended to make moral decisions based on what would best preserve relationships, and identified themselves in terms of their connectedness with others. Boys saw themselves as solitary individuals, while girls' identity was predicated on being part of a greater group.

Gilligan identified three stages in the development of this ethic of care, in response to Kohlberg's theory. The first level was where the individual cared only for herself. Moral decisions were based on what was good for the individual before others. The second level was where the individual saw virtue in caring for others. Self-sacrifice was seen as a virtue, but this wasn't a fully developed ethic of care. The third was where not only was there virtue in caring for others, but it is a universal imperative; caring for someone else was as morally important as caring for yourself.

Gilligan's work has been much discussed and much debated since. It came just towards the end of second wave feminism, asserting that while men and women were different, their strengths should be valued equally. It came just prior to the cusp of third wave feminism, which argued that the differences between men and women were fluctuating constantly and that nobody was 100 per cent male or 100 per cent female. Gilligan's work prompted the 'ethic of care' debate, which has been continuing for nigh on two decades now, pitting the ethic of justice against the ethic of care; the abstract against the contextualised, the principled against the non-principled, duty against care, and rights against responsibilities.

Much of the reforming work in Irish charity (that is, a move to offering more sustainable support) began in the 1980s, and research was conducted showing that there were five hundred homeless women in Dublin, where previously there were thought to be none. But whether this was prompted by a sisterly intention to help others (the 'universal imperative' described by Gilligan above) or an ethic of justice that wishes to see the same absolute rights afforded to all indiscriminately is immaterial. The fact remains that the result was a germination of future community building and that those connections, that 'web of life', will breed further connections. A holistic approach to the problems faced by the marginalised is an ethic of care that benefits all.

Such a holistic approach is one that could benefit feminism at large. Gilligan's analysis of moral development has been valuable, but perhaps the time has come to question whether viewing humankind in a gendered dichotomy has had its day. All ethical theories should really have a basis in experience, and experience tells us that although the individuals' view of the world are gendered, they're also influenced by a variety of other factors including race, age, socio-economic origin. It would be safe to say that my, albeit female, experience of the world has much more in common with white middle-class Irish males than it does, for example, with a female migrant worker in Ireland.

The Changing Irish Demographic

To suggest that it is women above any other group that are marginalised within Ireland is a fallacy. Our nation has long had a history of emigration, of Irish people leaving their homes to create new and perceived better lives for themselves in other countries, and now, for the first time in our history, we are faced with the reality of being so prosperous and wealthy a country that others leave their homes for a new and better life here. An entirely new class of potentially marginalised people now live in Ireland. The Irish society that existed twenty years ago is gone forever, and new challenges for care present themselves to us as the Irish environment continues to evolve.

The challenge that now faces Ireland is the challenge of multiculturalism, and just as Ireland now has to deal with the fact that there are more types of people than just men and women, so has feminism. It's a challenge that was laid down by many to argue against the essentially privileged ranks of academic feminism which initially failed to account for factors such as race; essentialising women as a unified, undifferentiated group.

Many authors have written about how feminism repeated the fundamental error of patriarchy in assuming that all women were the same, but the one that resonates with me quite closely is Donna J. Haraway.[3] She uses the model of a cyborg to describe the position of women today. A cyborg is neither fully human nor fully machine, and similarly women are neither fully defined by their femininity nor fully defined by their race, nor fully defined by their sexuality or their class background or their country of origin. We are partially defined by all these things, and more. In light of this, it's not legitimate to define a group of women as homogenous.

As I mentioned above, Irish society has changed, and changed forever. The details are as follows: between 1996 and 2002, Ireland had net immigration for the first time in history. Those figures show a net immigration of 26,000 (a figure roughly equivalent to the entire population of Drogheda). The 2002 census shows 224,261 'non-nationals' in Ireland (there was a total of 400,016 people who weren't born in Ireland).[4] This number is only going to grow. A report, 'Voices of Immigrants: The Challenges of Inclusion', published by the Immigrant Council of Ireland details some of the challenges of their immigration experiences. Just as Gilligan's report finally gave a voice to women's moral development, the ICI report gives a voice and story to immigrants in Ireland today. It contains fifteen recommendations of ways to fulfil the new needs created by the phenomenon of immigration, and at least some of them can only be fulfilled politically.

Politics and the 'Ethic of Care'

Many have taken Gilligan's initial research and used it to develop moral theory and ethics. Some, like Nel Noddings, a philosopher of education, came to emphasise the particularity of care. It disregards broad principles or rules of action, and at its root it places the immediate needs and concerns of human beings over abstract moral principles. The ethic of care takes each situation as it comes. Noddings differentiates between the cared-for and the caring individuals, and details how an ethic of care is relational and dependent. She also dismisses the possibility of using the ethic of care institutionally. By their very nature, institutions operate using abstract rules and principles, a 'one policy for everybody' principle that is fundamentally, according to Noddings, incompatible with an ethic of care. An institution can't act as one-caring, 'it can only capture what particular ones-caring would like to have done in well-described situations'.[6]

Joan C. Tronto, political scientist, would disagree.[7] She has written extensively on the implications of utilising the ethic of care politically throughout the 1980s and 1990s. She doesn't argue that morally speaking, an ethic of care is politically correct. She argues that politically speaking, an ethic of care is morally correct. The practice of using the ethic of care politically can only flourish after separating it from the gender dichotomy. If ethic of care research is conducted based on gender, then it should also involve class, racial and ethnic differences as well. Only then can it be developed as a moral theory for all.

Tronto departs from Noddings' description of a straightforward two-party relationship between the cared-for and the care-giver. Instead she argues that an ethic of care, while beginning with a willingness of suspend one's own goals and concerns in order to recognise others, has a greater potential. It is 'a species of activity that includes everything that we do to maintain, continue, and repair our 'world' so that we can live in it as well as possible.' Current political practices and social policy are mostly lacking in this ethos. She wishes to see political arenas 'value care and reshape institutions to reflect that changed value'.

Tronto doesn't argue that care should be a political ideal in all environments. She does argue that it can only flourish in liberal, pluralistic, democratic society. That, on paper at least, is what Ireland purports to be, so is there any way we could move forward with caring at our sails?

What Ireland Can Do

Immigration in Ireland today is an issue that can be used to demonstrate the areas in which Ireland could begin to utilise Tronto's concept of a caring political theory. As it currently stands, depending on what type of visa or permit is needed an individual may need to contact the Department of Justice, Equality and Law Reform, the Department of Enterprise, Trade and Employment, or the Department of Foreign Affairs. If that weren't confusing enough for the individual, they may also need to contact the Department of Social and Family Affairs, the Department of Education and Science, or many others before having completed the paperwork necessary for a move to Ireland. It may seem like a comical example of government buffoonery reminiscent of Terry Gilliam's *Brazil*, but the bureaucracy of it all belies a greater truth: there is little or no co-ordination between Government Departments on immigration policy, and there is no sustainable central government immigration policy at all. This will have to change.

The setting up of a cross-departmental mechanism (as the ICI suggested, a Ministry of State for Immigration and Ethnic Affairs) and the development of a comprehensive immigration policy is exactly what a state practising Tronto's political ethic of care would do.[8] It would be an acknowledgement of a need in our society. On one hand the state should do this because economically it's the right thing to do, Ireland's economy flourishes thanks to the toil of many immigrant workers, and skilled individuals will continue to be needed (cynically or not) as a means of production. But if the universal imperative to care stands within Irish society, a Ministry of State for Immigration would be able to meet the needs of information provision, develop a formal policy including family reunification, social inclusion, education, and a woman-positive policy including anti-trafficking measures. Such a Ministry would have to be sensitive and particularistic. If the EU can develop particular policies for particular situations (for example the upcoming directive on visas for victims of trafficking) then surely the Irish state can.[9] A neutral state can't act as an umpire on these issues.[10] We have to accept the indictment that as a nation we subject thousands to political indifference every day, and the time has come to accept the moral imperative to care.

Conclusion

The theories I have outlined above have developed in the academy over the past two decades, while some have been working in the real world to counter injustices we perpetrate on the homeless and the unfamiliar, the disadvantaged and the marginalised. While the 'ethic of care' debate has been raging among feminists and political scientists in journals and publications, real, life-changing care has been shown, promoted and implemented by projects run by agencies like Focus Ireland.

Whether this work is seen to fit into a feminist ethic of care and to promote a political theory of care, or if it is seen outside this framework entirely, is a matter of semantic bargaining. I merely wished to suggest one context among many from which we can view this work. Either way, this work, both at the coalface of charity and in social research informing health boards, social welfare and anti-racism policy stands as a testament to a career spent caring for others. Luke 14:13 contained a commitment to including the 'the poor, the lame, the maimed and the blind', and our challenge today is to adapt this Cecil B. DeMille version of injustice, with a particularity of care appropriate to our times, to include caring for the homeless, the displaced, the marginalised and (even still) the poor.

Notes

1. Carol Gilligan, *In a Different Voice: Psychological Theory and Women's Development* (Cambridge: Harvard University Press, 1982).
2. Lawrence Kohlberg, *The Philosophy of Moral Development: Moral Stages and The Idea of Justice* (London: Harper & Row, 1981).
3. Donna J. Harway, 'Manifesto for Cyborgs: Science Technology, and Socialist Feminism in the 1980s,' *Socialist Review* no. 80: 65-108. Since developed and republished as 'A Cyborg Manifesto: Science Technology and Socialist-Feminism in the Late Twentieth Century,' In *Simians, Cyborgs and Women: The Reinvention of Nature*, ed. Donna J. Haraway (London: Free Association Books, 1991), 183-202.
4. Census 2002, Central Statistics Office. Available online at: http://www.cso.ie/census.html
5. Kelleher Associates, *Voices of Immigration: The Challenges of Inclusion* (Dublin: Immigrant Council of Ireland, 2004).
6. Nel Noddings, *Women and Evil* (Berkley: University of California Press, 1989), 103.
7. Joan C. Tronto, 'Beyond Gender Difference to a Theory of Care', In *An Ethic of Care: Feminist and Interdisciplinary Perspectives*, ed. M.J. Larrabee. (London: Routledge, 1993), 240-258.
8. Kelleher Associates, *Voices*, 82.
9. The EU Parliament has approved, with a number of proposed amendments, the Council's Directive on short term permits for victims of trafficking. The proposed amendments include the insertion of a statutory thirty day reflection period for victims of trafficking. Full text and proposed amendments available online at: http://www3.europarl.eu.int/omk/omisapir.so/pv2?PRG=QUERY &APP=PV2&LANGUE=EN&TYPEF=A5&FILE=BIBLIO04&NU MERO=0099&YEAR=04
10. Joan C. Tronto, *Moral Boundaries: A Political Argument for An Ethic of Care* (London: Routledge, 1993), 92.

THE DINNER

Brendan Kennelly

*Jesus himself showed the importance of an 'ethic of care' in the way
he washed the apostles' feet at the Last Supper. Jesus sat down to have
meals with a number of different people, and it is noteworthy in the
contemporary context that many of them, like the tax-collector, were
on the margins of society. In his humorous poem 'The Dinner'
Brendan Kennelly imagines what might have happened if James Joyce
had been a guest at a meal of the Holy Family.*

James Joyce had dinner with the Holy Family
One Saturday evening in Nazareth.
Mary was a good cook, her Virginsoup was delicious,
Joyce lapped it till he was nearly out of breath.
The Holy Family looked at Joyce who said
Nothing, he was a morose broody class
Of a man, his glasses made him look very sad,
It was next to impossible to get him to talk and
The dinner was uncomfortable as a result.
'How're things in Ireland?' asked Joseph. 'Ugh,' said Joyce.
'What're you writing now?' persisted Joseph, 'I couldn't find fault

With your last book. Perfect.'

Joyce seemed to sulk.

'A large work,' he muttered, 'Like the Bible. The sea. My voices.'

'Am I in it?' queried Jesus. 'Yep,' said Joyce. 'Pass the salt.'

'Is it too much to enquire about the role I play?'

Continued Jesus. 'It is,' said Joyce.

Mary changed the subject. 'Are there many grottoes to me

In Ireland?' 'Countless,' replied the hero.

Joyce's short answers were buggering the dinner up.

'The Society of Jesus,' queried Jesus, 'How's it going?'

'Who knows Clongowes?' said Joyce. 'Could I have a cup

Of Bewley's coffee to round off this occasion?'

'Why did you leave Ireland, James?' queried Joseph,

'The Swiss, French, Italians are just as lousy

In their ways.' Joyce pondered. 'Crime,'

He replied, 'Of non-being.' Jesus butted in:

'In that case you must have sinners in plenty.

I think I should visit Ireland, sometime.'

'I wouldn't, if I were you,' said Joyce.

'But you're not me,' said Jesus. 'Though there

Are times when you behave as if you were

The Son of Man Himself. You get in my hair,

James, from time to time, with your pretentious

Posturing, sitting on a cloud, paring your toenails

In an orgy of indifference, pissed on white wine.

Though I readily admit your prose is divine

With touches of Matthew Mark Luke and John,

Why can't you be an honest-to-God

Dubliner, go for a swim in Sandymount, spend
Sunday afternoon in Croke Park or Dalyer,
Boast of things you've never done,
Places you've never been,
Have a pint in O'Neill's,
Misjudge the political scene,
Complain about the weather,
Miss mass, go to Knock,
Take a week in Killarney,
Listen to McCormack's records,
Re-learn to mock, jibe, scandalise, sneer, scoff
And talk your head off.
James, you have a block about Ireland,
You're too long on the continent.
In some strange way, James, you are,
If you ask me, bent.'

'But I didn't ask you, Jesus,' replied Joyce,
'It so happens I think things out for myself,
I had to leave Ireland to do this
Because no one in Ireland has a mind of his own,
I know that place to the marrow of its bone
And I insist that people are dominated by your henchmen,
Those chaps in black who tell folk what to think.'

'I beg your pardon,' said Jesus 'These men
Are not me.'

'Would you put that in ink?'
Asked Joyce.
'In blood,' Jesus replied.

'This is getting too serious,' Joseph interrupted.

'Shut up, Dad!' said Jesus. 'The matter *is* serious.
It's precisely for this kind of crap I came and died.'

'But you're alive and well, son,' Joseph said. 'You're not dead
And we're the Holy Family. That's what they call us.'

'What family is wholly holy?' asked Jesus.
Joseph looked about him, then at the ground, perplexed.
That honest carpenter didn't seem comfortable.

There was nothing he couldn't to with timber
But this was a different matter.

He said nothing,
Just poured himself another cup of Bewley's coffee.
Mary said, 'Let's finish with a song,
Mr Joyce, I understand that you
Took second place
To Mr McCormack at a Feis.
But that's a long time ago, a long
Time ago.
Though second place is not the place for you
Perhaps you'd give the Holy Family a song.'

Joyce brooded a bit, took a deep breath,
Straightened his glasses gone slightly askew,
Coughed once, then sang *The Rose of Nazareth*.

The Holy Family loved his voice.
It was pure and clear and strong,
The perfect voice of the perfect sinner

And the perfect end to the dinner.

RESURRECTION IN A HOLE OF MUD

Alice Taylor

*In a very personal contribution Alice Taylor reminds us, in prose and
poetry, that Easter is a time of resurrection and the divine entering the
human.*

It was a cold wet Easter Saturday morning. On a muddy hill
outside the village a small group of us planted trees. As we dug
holes we sank into the surrounding mud. We had considered
cancelling the outing but it was the only Saturday on which we
were all available and the young trees were bare-rooted and
needed to go into the earth. So we had decided to forge ahead
regardless of the weather, which was ferocious.

As the morning wore on light-hearted banter was eroded by
the gruelling conditions. Hunched figures dug determinedly as
faces tinged navy blue and fingers numbed under steely rain.
But a silent determination prevailed. The silence suited me; it
flowed like a grey cloak over my bereaved mind.

A few weeks previously someone very close to me had died
suddenly and the sunny meadow of my mind had been
ploughed up and turned into a field of thorns. Now as I dug
and planted, warm tears ran silently down my frozen face. I
became part of the blinding rain. Slowly my mind evaporated

and the whole world turned into digging and planting. I dragged my heavy boots out of the sunken holes of sucking mud. There was not time, only mud and rain.

Hours later all was planted. I trudged home stiff and exhausted. As I peeled off my muddy boots I wondered if my frozen body would ever thaw or my stiff joints ever turn freely again. My body was exhausted but for some unexplainable reason my mind, for the first time in months, felt better than my body. Some resurrection had begun. Was there, I wondered, healing in the earth?

During the following months I went out daily and dug the earth and created a new garden. Each time, the earth absorbed a little more of my pain and slowly over the months healing gradually began to take place. It took no effort on my part only the willingness to go out and dig and plant. The rest was up to the creativity of creation. I discovered that creation could recreate a devastated mind.

Now four years later I watch those trees grow stronger and I know that on that Easter Saturday morning with the planting of those little trees on that muddy hill my resurrection from bereavement began.

PEOPLE OF GOLD

Alice Taylor

They sat in a circle
People from homes
Of ailing, old
And fettered young
These were the carers
Who gave long hours
Of unceasing dedication
To limited family lives
That sucked the energy
From their days and nights

I was doing a reading
For these people of kindness
My inadequate words
Washed around these rocks
Of solid gold.

UPLIFT

Alice Taylor

'Fruits of the earth
And work of human hands'
Today I heard
For the first time
Saw the climb
The earth,
The human,
The divine.

A MESSAGE OF HOPE

Trevor Sargent

One of the blots on the Irish landscape is the damage we have done to our environment. Arguably the environmental destruction is but a symptom of a deeper underlying spiritual crisis or even a metaphor for the human condition. In persisting to damage our environment we are showing our contempt for God's good creation. Trevor Sargent's piece reminds us of the link between the hope of Easter and our duty to care for the earth.

The message of Easter is at once powerful, joyous and hopeful. Rising up to overcome pain, laying down a formula of justice, equality and peace. Putting in place prayerful support structures to help each other where help is needed. All this to me in the face of any challenge gives hope – the hope which Jesus Christ makes a realisation at Easter.

Many positions Jesus took and statements he made are still seen as revolutionary and were especially so in the context of the society into which he was born. So revolutionary in bringing justice 'on Earth as it is in Heaven' that the message is still too hot to handle for some.

Jesus, I believe, came to extend the circle of ethics as wide as possible. Beyond Jewish people, beyond white people, beyond people altogether. Why else would Jesus tell us to 'go into the world and preach the good news to all creation'? (Mark 16:15)

St Paul reflected this inclusive and wide circle of ethics also in his letter to the Colossians, 1:19-20 declaring 'for God was pleased to have all his fullness dwell in Christ, and through Christ to reconcile to himself all things, whether things on earth or things in heaven, by making peace through his blood shed on the cross'.

Failure to reconcile humankind to the carrying capacity of the earth and the obscene lack of equity in how resources are distributed is certainly storing up trouble. The symptoms of climate change are not just climatic records of hurricanes and high tides. The tide of refugees displaced by environmental crises is also on the rise. So great is this tide of human misery that the UNHCR sees no option but to plead poverty itself and continue in denial of environmental refugees – restricting its resources for refugees displaced by war and other such 'conventional' political problems.

My hope is that very soon the penny will drop that to distinguish 'conventional' from 'environmental' refugees is as unjustifiable as apartheid between people of different races or ethnic backgrounds.

Job in the Old Testament fell into the trap of taking nature for granted, treating the non-human parts of God's creation as being of lesser importance than him; God, the egalitarian, non-speciest Creator sets out to change Job's tune. Can Job be helped to live in harmony with the life support systems of planet Earth?

Whatever about a message of hope for the present day challenges facing all Easter people, it seems humankind is all too often destined to learn the hard way.

THE HABIT OF REDEMPTION

Brendan Kennelly

Redemption is at the heart of the mystery of Easter. Brendan Kennelly's poem 'The Habit of Redemption' reminds us of the importance of redemption.

I have felt the world shrivel to days
Beckoning me
Into a hell of indifference

Until I found
The habit of redemption
Living in my mind.

It breathed in the morning
As I wrote a letter
To a woman in mourning

For her dead brother.
He was sixty-six
And rare,

His days touched by imagination.
He died in October
Tending his garden.

It reached the deepest part of me
When the middle-aged man
Raking leaves turned quickly

And said 'how are you?'
Autumn died at his feet
But the day was new.

I would say nothing about all this,
Never bother to mention
The moment's metamorphosis

Were it not that hell gapes
At every step.
What I am given is not a means of escape

But of confrontation,
The truest education
That I know.

Moment that is all moments
Be with me when I grasp
A little of the meaning of transience,

A hint of the infernal night.
Come in the shape of a blade of grass
Stuck to the side of my boot

Or a kind word from stranger or friend
Or a yellow shedding from an old tree
That will not bend.

GOOD NEWS

John Scally

If the problem of Ireland today is that we only pay lip-service to the Christianity we claim to worship, part of the solution must be to re-learn and re-discover the beauty and majesty of the language of Christianity which is the language of love. In this vision what we really need is for the creative transformative potential of Christian love to invade the barren sterility of our lives, in all its dimensions, 'sacred and profane'. The final article considers the implications of living as Easter people amidst the pain and confusion of our sometimes troubled existence, insofar as the Resurrection, with its pledge of a liberating love that brings forth new life animates our thoughts, words and actions.

When I was a young boy my grandfather told me the story of a man who had lived in our village. During the Great Famine he was one of the seven local men who were hanged for stealing on Good Friday. Six bags of potatoes were stolen from the pit of the local landlord. Six local men with large families and no food had crept into Lord McNocholas' farmyard and stolen a bag each, but the man who was punished had done no wrong. This poignant story of an innocent man unjustly hanged for the failures of others enabled me to think of Good Friday in an emotionally significant and humanising way.

To be honest I needed something like that to change my childhood perception that the God of Good Friday was really a tyrannical figure who demanded the violent death of his only Son in order to put the world, which had gone wrong, right again. With maturity I came to realise that God did not want the violent death of Jesus; rather He wanted the total response of the Son. God accepts the self-sacrifice of Jesus's death because of the potential it entails for both His glorification and our glorification.

Good Friday is the day which the Christian Church has designated as the time we remember in a special way those we have loved and lost. It is a day which we in Ireland have historically marked by visits to the local Church for services, like the Stations of the Cross. I still recall from my childhood three altar boys journeying with the priest as he walked solemnly to each of the stations, two carried candles, and one a big wooden cross. Then the priest forcefully boomed out the chant at each station:

O Jesus for love of me did'st bear thy cross to Calvary
In thy sweet mercy grant me to suffer and to die with thee.

Those lines penetrated my brain and did not give me a sense of the debt all Christians owed to the Saviour. Good Friday is both a richly communal event and a uniquely personal one when we remember our own dark days of grief, sadness and incalculable loss.

When every day is Good Friday

My mother's voice was fractured with emotion as she spoke down the crackling line. Although her voice was scarcely audible her words are forever imprinted in my memory: 'Prepare yourself for an awful shock. Are you sitting down?' The blackest possible scenarios exploded through my brain. Except that one. 'Poor Oliver got a heart-attack this morning and died in Betie's shed. The ambulance came and took him away. Can you come home?'

The foundations I thought were firm under my feet had crumbled. Oliver, was my best friend. My next door neighbour. My cousin. My soulmate. I've been told that from a certain angle we could have been mistaken for twins. He was the brother I never had. The finality of his death hit home with brutal force. From then on I would have to think of him in the past tense.

I braced myself for the saddest moment of my life when I arrived at his house. It was a weird experience to walk through the door. I wanted to turn back but something inside me kept me walking on. I had expected to see his body in the living room. I had tried to prepare myself for this moment. But when I realised his corpse was but feet away from me, it was frightening in the extreme. I went to offer words of consolation to his family – but it was they who comforted me.

My mind was spinning with questions. Oliver was just thirty-three years of age. I could not comprehend why his radiant eyes had to surrender their sight. Nor why his articulate voice had to give away its speech. Justice should not allow the sacrifice of such innocent wealth.

Well meaning sympathisers trotted out soothing phrases: 'It's God's holy will.' Right then I wished God had never been invented. Another said: 'It's happy for him. There's something beautiful about a young death.' Happy, beautiful? I wanted to scream at such a perversion of language. But it was not the time nor the place nor did I have the energy. I am not sure why but I felt compelled to touch his forehead. The coldness of death repelled me and I pulled back my hand immediately. For the first time I discovered that tears tasted of salt.

On the third day Oliver was buried. His funeral was a very moving occasion. The grief though intensely personal was generously shared. The local community always responded magnificently in times of adversity. Everyone rallied around. Every seat in the house was crammed with relatives and neighbours, all with mournful faces. They had good reason to in this court of human suffering. The next hour or so disappeared in a complete haze as if I'd lost a piece of my life. A few drops of rain fell. I suspected they were tears of anger for a deed both wrong and absurd.

Oliver was laid to rest in an austere ceremony. Tradition in rural Roscommon dictated that the nearest neighbours – on the prompting of the bereaved – dig the grave and later fill the clay over the coffin with a sense of privilege and decorum. The frozen clay seemed to resent the willing shovels. There was a finality about the proceedings in the tap-tap-tap as the back of the spade shaped the remaining mounds of fresh clay. What really crucified me though was the sound of clods of earth crashing on the coffin. Now we will be forever friends in two different worlds.

I waited until the mourners had departed because I wanted to be alone with him for a final moment. I prayed to buy him some shares in the hereafter. Now I know why 'Goodbye' is the most painful word in the English language. Parting is no sweet sorrow. At that moment the sun came out of hiding like a scene from an autumnal coloured photograph. The symbol surely was the reality. Oliver had risen with the Son.

Paradise Regained

Good Friday reminds us that Paradise Lost is only one half of the story, Paradise Regained is the other. This is the day when the Church invites us to reflect on the mystery of death itself. It is an invitation I, for one, am reluctant to take up as the thought of death sends a chill to my bones but I feel it is my duty to Oliver to do so. The sadness of Oliver's death will always remain with me. This day the Christian Church challenges me to integrate this experience into my life, rather than engaging in escapism or falling prey to despair: to find something constructive in this most destructive experience of our human existence. To do this I must interpret the meaning of Oliver's death in the light of the life, death and Resurrection of Jesus Christ.

Jesus was really dead. His death was never undone. The Resurrection did not negate Jesus's death because as a gracious act of God it is only possible once all human freedom and power have come to a complete and irreversible end in death. Jesus maintained his complete commitment to his Father's will even when he confronted the certitude of his personal extinction. In raising Jesus from the dead God has not undone the laws of nature. Instead the Father has manifested his fidelity to his son by accepting the total self-giving and accompanying powerlessness of Jesus at the cross and by glorifying Jesus as the first-born of a new eternal order of relationships as they are meant to be.

In the words of St Paul: 'Do you not know that all of us who have been baptised into Christ Jesus were baptised into his death? Therefore we have been buried with him by baptism into death, so that, just as Christ was raised from the dead by the glory of the Father, so we too might walk in newness of life.' (Rom 6:3-4) In this perspective eternal life starts now. It is the quality of God's relationship to us and God's fidelity to us which gifts us with eternal life in the here and now. Accordingly, while death is the end of our life it is not the end of our story. Death is a new beginning: an opening to the consummation of a new relationship with God which has already begun in this life. It is hard to equate Good Friday in our minds with Good News but we should. In the words of Abelard's lovely Good Friday hymn we see:

> the Lord gone for the sacrifice
> so that we too can win the laughter of thine Easter day.

Today the cross remains as a poignant, and appropriate, reminder of a man who embodied the Christian virtue of loving without counting the cost and who tragically paid the ultimate price. Through this cross a man long dead lives again, somehow speaking through the years that belong to people not yet born.

The Ignored Day

It is easy to talk about love, but more difficult to live it as Jesus himself found out. As a boy the one thing I never understood was why we had to bother going to Church on Easter Saturday when nothing really happened on that day. On Good Friday we are asked, 'Were you there when they crucified my Lord?' It is an uncomfortable question and one most of us would rather avoid. Jesus died and is buried and all is apparently over. On Easter Sunday we marvel at the miraculous. The crucified Jesus has unexpectedly become the risen Christ. The eternal has invaded the transient. The Jesus of Good Friday has shown once for all that God's relationship with each of us transcends the limitations of this life. But why waste time with Easter Saturday when Jesus is just napping in the tomb?

Holy Saturday is a day of waiting, not for God, but on God. It is a day not about our experience but Jesus', his descent into hell as it were, opening up a way for us through the very powers that would otherwise destroy us. As an integral, though neglected, component of the Paschal Mystery, it evokes a faithful waiting on God in the darkness of faith and invites a spirituality of silence. Only in silence and contemplation can we allow God to reveal the divine greatness to us.

Growing up on a sheep farm in Roscommon I never failed to get a little thrill from bringing a lamb into the world, especially after a very difficult birth. I felt I was part, in some way, of achieving the miracle of new life.

Once I witnessed the dawn breaking as I went to check on a sickly lamb. A tumult of sound greeted me, every bird in the fields singing its heart out, although it was still dark. Gradually the sky lightened and the low bruised clouds began to be caressed with red. Then for a few moments the birds fell silent. The carollers drew close and paused to seek out instruments, searching for the string, the bow, the drum, to make the appropriate melody. That was the instant the sun appeared over the horizon. The birds went silent with the wonder that was the only possible response. Praise was secondary. It seemed that all of nature was affected by a tremor of excitement, adoring the creator. Timelessness breathed through the daybreak like the heartbeat of a new baby.

When the birds began to sing again, it was not the pre-dawn hubbub at all, but something more reverential like a heavenly choir. Subtle tunes resonated with ancient harmonies. It was like the first music ever made. All life was simplified. All thoughts were complete. Music was the best for this. The words of everyday are unworthy vehicles to describe the transcendent. I now realise that this shock and awe was theological reflection at its most eloquent: a glorious tribute to the wonder of God. This opened my eyes to the rich mysteries of the real presence. Through this experience I would later understand why Patrick Kavanagh would react against an over-institutionalised religion which failed to see Christ outside the institutional structures:

> Yet sometimes when the sun comes through a gap
> These men know God the Father in a tree:
> The Holy Spirit in the rising sap,
> and Christ will be the green leaves that come
> At Easter from the sealed and guarded tomb.

Easter Saturday is the day we are given the breathing space to prepare for the real presence. It is a gentle call to slow down and reflect on the bigger picture. Who is the God of the Paschal Mystery for us today?

This is a lull before the Easter storm when we remember our call to bear witness to a Christianity which has a vital, personal quality rather than being something worn ostentatiously like a religious emblem and a spirituality that is deep, mysterious and beautiful, a religion that gives sympathy to our hearts and understanding to our minds.

Holy Saturday is a day when, more than any other, we are aware of the life that makes us live, the expectation of a new beginning, new birth and hope and the inexhaustible, now accessible divine potential that is all around us. It is a welcome opportunity to savour the energy, joy, and trust of the unique Easter laughter. It is also a day when we are particularly conscious of the wisdom of Brendan Kennelly's words, 'Self knows that self is not enough.'

Accordingly, the Easter mystery challenges us to joyfully embrace an ethic of community and to work for justice. This is a Good News we do not just talk about. It is a Good News we live. It is a particular kind of Good News because its truth hurts as much as it liberates. Sadly there are many cosy corners that need to be challenged and many aspects of Irish society that stand in need of liberation.

Amongst Women

Ezra Pound's quotation is to me a brilliant summary of the Christian life: 'Nothing matters but the quality of the affection – in the end – that has carved the trace in the mind.' The church which Jesus called for was a radical presence which empowered all people to have meaningful life.

A Christianity which is audible without being visible is a counter-sacrament. If Irish Christianity today is to regain its credibility it must forge a new alliance with the poor and marginalised. It must be bold enough to be baptised in the Jordan of the real state of Irish religion and courageous enough to be baptised on the cross of Irish poverty and social exclusion. Our search for the Irish face of Christ can not be authentic until we honestly confront the social structures and attitudes that cause some people to feel that there is no room for them at the inn.

Jesus formulated an alternative model of society. This Christ exalted even on the Cross, healed the broken, fed the multitudes, and significantly removed social stigmas (leprosy) and reintegrated outcasts like prostitutes and tax-collectors into society. We in Ireland could best put the Christ back into Irish Christianity by integrating the outcasts in Irish society.

The noted Jewish philosopher, Emmanuel Levinas, has argued persuasively that God created people because he wanted someone to speak with. This was why his Word had to be made flesh. St John's Gospel announces with a flourish: 'The Word was made flesh'. With one fell swoop we learn from this dramatic and almost incomprehensible revelation of the immense love of God. The incarnation turned the ways of the world on its head. After this event glory is to be found in humiliation, riches in poverty and, most strangely of all, life in death.

It is for this reason that St Paul can say that the Word came in the flesh of sin, under the law, like a slave, and under the power of death. His 'failure' and final humiliation began the moment he was received by Mary. Jesus took on a human form so that we might find him in others. The tragic parts of our human existence, our poverty and weakness, our sickness, darkness and death have all being graced by the presence of Jesus. All the darkest forces of the human condition are now basically filled with the truth of his life, with his freedom that is authentic freedom, with the majesty of his power. We do not have to seek God any more in the celestial heavens. Jesus has come right here among us. He is sharing our burden, has tasted the bitterness of our life, has travelled our highways and by ways.

Through the incarnation a new heaven, a new earth was created. A new force and spirit has entered the world – light, love, wisdom and joy have entered the human heart and mind, and in the eyes of God, a new springtime has begun in all of creation. From Mary's humanity, she gave him his humanity. Every heartbeat of hers gave him a heart to love with. The ordinary has become the extraordinary and the extraordinary has become ordinary.

This insight reminds us that God is a living God, someone who loves people and loves to be loved by people. It is not humankind who is waiting for God, but God who is waiting for us. Of course this leaves God vulnerable because effectively the future is surrendered to us. Jesus did not come to condemn or to pontificate, but to show what it means to be truly human. He came with a promise, 'I come that you may have life and have it to the full.' In the Gospel we find Jesus repeating over and over again the simple advice, 'Watch and pray'.

This was not merely a readiness for unexpected death. It is far wider than that. It is to be alert to the call of God in one's immediate situation. To take this journey of God with humanity gives people the possibility of fullness of life. In the encounter with God-with-us, God-for-us, women and men come to a fuller understanding of God, of themselves of the meaning and purpose of life. Throughout the Old Testament and the letters of Paul and his companions, indeed the Gospels themselves, account after account occurs of the way in which God has broken into the lives of women and men while they were journeying, utterly transforming their awareness of themselves, their understanding of live, their appreciation of God, and through that experience giving them a broader vision of the character of the people of God. One of the characteristic notes of the Gospels is the invitation issued by Jesus to women and men, 'Follow Me'. This following involves renouncing of the disciples previous security – the security of the known, and the committing of the disciple to the unknown. The invitation of Jesus to 'Follow Me' was regarded as imperative if the fullness of life were to be embraced.

Discipleship involves moving from one mode of life to another, from one set of values to another, from one way of acting to another, and from a life circumscribed by family and friends to a life in community with women and men of diverse backgrounds and expectations. This journey brings difficulties:

trials, temptations, the yearnings for the security of the known and tried, yet it is only as the pilgrim faces these temptations and leaves behind the security of the known that the way itself becomes clear.

This journey is not just for a disparate group of individuals but by people who are part of a corporate body. The biblical images are images of the community. It is evident that Israel is a people on a journey, a community learning from their conventional relationship with God, revising and enlarging their understanding as the pilgrim people of God. The Christian life is a communal adventure, a voyage of discovery, a journey, sustained by faith and hope. Today we are challenged to make great efforts to take such a journey together. As we co-operate in trying to clarify our mission we are learning from each other, and producing insights which are richer and more complete than those arrived at in our separate existences. In theological terms we become 'partners in conversation'.

In the Bible the question of where and how we can serve the Lord has an unambiguous answer. We find him in the hungry, the thirsty, the stranger and the naked, we see him wherever people are in need and cry out for help. The Christian God revealed to humankind in a definitive way in the bruised and broken body of the suffering Jesus, continues to reveal himself wherever human suffering is to be found. From the beginning Christians were people who recognised God in the course of their daily care of others. The heart of their discipleship was the ongoing discovery of God's presence in the midst of the human struggle.

Despite our pain and difficulties our faith insulates us from the danger of being totally overwhelmed by our problems and ensures that the disappointments and disillusionments of our daily lives do not narrow our vision nor blind us to anything beyond our own problems. Our care for those on the margins and the poor reveals the deep connections of our individual lives with the saving life of Jesus Christ. This requires action on the socio-political level.

The God of the Easter story is an impatient figure, hungry to transform us into worthy bearers of the name 'Christian'. It is through love alone that we please God and our main challenge is to acquire that love. Christians best respond to the invitation of Jesus to love not by building memorials to the dead but by giving food to the living. The secret of life is that only in love for the living is the spirit praised forever. Our challenge at Easter and every day is to allow this love to be a lamp for our steps and a light for our eyes as we understand God's call to us in terms of a movement towards a participatory community between human beings and God, which allows all life to unfold its divinely inspired development.

Jesus came on earth to love and be loved. The Christian life is an exchange of love – the love we receive and the love we give for Christ. To walk the way of unconditional love is to accept an arduous task. This is both the challenge and the invitation Jesus gives to all of us to be Easter people.

BEGIN

Brendan Kennelly

In the final scene of the medieval epic La Chanson de Roland *the great Christian hero Charlemagne sat exhausted in Aix, his battles with the Moors over. According to the poem, he was more than nine hundred years old. An angel wakened the old man from his sleep and told him to get up again and return to battle because the work should not be finished until the end of time. Charlemagne sighed: 'Dieu, si penuse est ma vie. (O God how hard is my life.)' The work of the here remains unfinished, but who will do it if not he or she? Accordingly, we conclude with Brendan Kennelly's uplifting, yet challenging, poem 'Begin' which reminds us that the work of an Easter people must continue until the very last day.*

Begin again to the summoning birds
to the sight of light at the window,
begin to the roar of morning traffic
all along Pembroke Road.
Every beginning is a promise
born in light and dying in dark
determination and exaltation of springtime
flowering the way to work.
Begin to the pageant of queuing girls

the arrogant loneliness of swans in the canal
bridges linking the past and future
old friends passing though with us still.
Begin to the loneliness that cannot end
since it perhaps is what makes us begin,
begin to wonder at unknown faces
at crying birds in the sudden rain
at branches stark in the willing sunlight
at seagulls foraging for bread
at couples sharing a sunny secret
alone together while making good.
Though we live in a world that dreams of ending
that always seems about to give in
something that will not acknowledge conclusion
insists that we forever begin.

I Believe

by John Scally

ISBN: 1 85390 598 4

Twenty-one interviews conducted by John Scally, producer of the hugely popular radio programme, **I Believe**, brought together here to engage and entertain. Interviewees include Joseph O'Connor, Jimmy Magee, Alice Taylor and Sr Helen Prejean.

VERITAS

DOCTOR'S ORDERS?

Towards a New Medical
Ethics

John Scally

ISBN: 1 85390 582 8

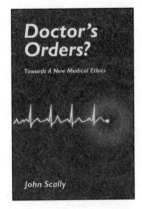

In *Doctor's Orders?* John Scally takes a critical look at the medical profession and concludes that the time has come for a radical cultural change in the practice of medicine in Ireland. In our era of transparency he calls for a more accountable profession where doctors face up to their responsibilities to society. He also outlines the need for greater equity in the allocation of resources in health care. In our Celtic Tiger prosperity how can we allow our two-tier health care system to continue any longer?

Doctor's Orders? is packed with the accounts of people who have suffered at the hands of the medical profession in Ireland. Anyone who reads their harrowing testimonies will be convinced of the need for radical surgery in the medical profession and not just a 'band-aid' solution.

An invaluable and thought-provoking book for anyone interested in health and the medical profession.